JESUS ... *my final answer*

~

Kenny Ashley

Copyright © 2007 by Kenny Ashley

Jesus... My Final Answer
by Kenny Ashley

Printed in the United States of America

ISBN 978-1-60266-715-0

All rights reserved solely by the author. The author guarantees all contents are original and do not infringe upon the legal rights of any other person or work. No part of this book may be reproduced in any form without the permission of the author. The views expressed in this book are not necessarily those of the publisher.

Unless otherwise indicated, Bible quotations are taken from the NEW LIVING TRANSLATION of the Bible. Copyright © 1996 by Tyndale Charitable Trust.

Bible quotations marked NIV are taken from the NEW INTERNATIONAL VERSION of the Bible. Copyright © 1973, 1978, 1984 by International Bible Society. Used by permission of Zondervan Publishing House.

Bible quotations marked KJV are taken from the KING JAMES VERSION of the Bible.

Bible quotations marked NKJV are taken from the NEW KING JAMES VERSION of the Bible. Copyright © 1982 by Thomas Nelson, Inc.

Bible quotations marked AMP are taken from THE AMPLIFIED BIBLE, Old Testament. Copyright © 1965, 1987 by the Zondervan Corporation. The Amplified New Testament copyright © 1958, 1987 by the Lockman Foundation. Used by permission.

www.xulonpress.com

Dedication

To my precious daughter, **Kia**, whose name means, "a season of new beginnings." Twenty-three years ago, you brought a season of joy into my life that has had no end… only beginnings. I love you, Baby Girl!

Special Thanks

To Jesus Who is, and always will be, MY Final Answer.

To Nana who now watches over me from her home in heaven with Jesus.

To Pop who is the greatest Dad, friend and encourager I know.

Preface

Whatever we do, it is because Christ's love controls us.
—2 Corinthians 5:14 NLT

Is Jesus your final answer? Does His love, and His love alone, control you? Have you surrendered your life... your dreams... your hopes... your desires... your whole being to Christ? If not, you are not controlled by His love. You are controlled by your own agenda. Your motives are impure. You serve to fulfill your life, not to glorify His.

If you are serving others for any other motivation than honoring the Lord, your service will always have limits. There are some things you may do for others, but some things you won't do. There was nothing Jesus would not do for us if His Father asked Him to do it. He was obedient even to the point of death... even the death on the cross (Philippians 2:8).

Mary Magdalene was tormented for years by seven demons. One day Father God said, **"Enough is enough! Son, set her free!"** And Jesus served His Father and obeyed. He cast those demons out of Mary, and her life was changed forever. After that fateful day, there was nothing she would not do for Jesus. No task was too menial. His love controlled her.

Mary's life drastically changed forever because she knew something most people do not know. She knew... really knew how desperately hopeless and helpless she was. She knew she was nothing. She knew she had nothing. Therefore, she knew she had nothing to lose. Jesus was not only her *final* answer, He was her *only* answer.

Beloved, that is the place where you will find all you've been looking for. Seven demons brought Mary to the place in her life where Jesus was her only hope. Who, or what, is escorting you? Sickness? A broken relationship? Divorce? A haunting past? Regret? Fear? Doubt? Confusion? Emptiness? Loneliness?...

Take heart! Those things are not menaces. They are golden chariots propelling you to the place where Hopelessness intersects with the Way, the Truth and the Life. When you reach that point, any way you turn will lead you Home!

1

Ask Me and I will tell you some remarkable secrets about what is going to happen here. — Jeremiah 33:3 NLT

Henry Blackaby, the author of <u>**Experiencing God**</u>, said that we often get the wrong answer because we ask the wrong question. The wrong question: *"What is God's will for my life?"* The right question: *"What is God's will?"* Do you see the difference? The first question is self-centered. It revolves around *my* finding out what I'm supposed to be doing and then getting God to come help me accomplish *my* plan. The second question is God-centered. It seeks to find out what God is doing and then asking how I can help Him accomplish *His* plans.

Today, we want to ask some right questions in hopes that we can know and understand that He is the Final Answer. Think about these and ask **The Final Answer** to direct your thoughts.

> Do you need a good swift kick in your "can'ts"?
> Do you count your blessings, or do you think your blessings don't count?
> What good is aim if you never pull the trigger?
> Are you known by the promises you don't keep?

Have you noticed that 99% of the things you worry
  about never happen?
Are you a winner, or a whiner?
Do you make promises, or commitments?
Do you believe your doubts and doubt your beliefs?
Have you been ignoring the still small Voice inside
  of you? What is He saying?
Are you making a cemetery out of your life by
  burying your talents and gifts?
Are you always getting ready to live, but never
  getting around to living?
What far-reaching effects could be realized if you
  recognized the purpose God has for you, and
  you started today to work toward that purpose?
Is your fear of loss greater than your desire to
  glorify God?
Do you let God heal your hurts, or do you memorize
  them?
If you had the power to do anything, how would
  you go about deciding what to do?
If not you, then who? If not now, then when?
Are you willing to give up what you have and who
  you are to gain what God wants to give you and
  to be who He wants you to be?
What is most important to you in life?
Is that your Final Answer?

"Heavenly Father, I know the answers You want to hear, but they are not always the answers I want to give. I'll admit that I am still a little self-centered. I still whine when I don't get my way. My heart's desire is for Jesus to be my Final Answer for all of life's questions. Would You help me ask the right questions? Would You keep me reaching for my destiny... the destiny You put inside of me? You are the best, Lord. Amen."

2

So don't worry about tomorrow, for tomorrow will bring its own worries. Today's trouble is enough for today.
— Matthew 6:34 NLT

I'm a pragmatist. I'm one of those people who approach life and its problems in a logical, practical and systematic way. My life has always been filled with *"One day I'm going to..."* and *"Maybe someday I'll..."* and *"When I get a chance, I'm..."* As you well know, those times never come. So you just keep walking that mundane treadmill we've come to know as life doing the same old, same old all the time. But I'm not getting any younger. I'm convinced that Jesus died to give us life to live and enjoy, not to endure. I'm learning to "chill out" and take time to smell the roses instead of worrying so much about avoiding the thorns. I found this little story to be a confirmation of my new approach to living rather than merely existing. I hope it does the same for you.

My brother-in-law opened the bottom drawer of my sister's bureau and lifted out a tissue-wrapped package. *"This,"* he said, *"is not a slip. This is lingerie."* He discarded the tissue and handed me the slip. It was exquisite... silk, handmade and trimmed with a cobweb of lace. The price tag with an astronomical figure on it was still attached. *"Jan bought this the first time we went to New York, at least 8 or 9 years ago. She never wore it. She was saving it for a special occasion. Well, I guess this is the occasion."*

He took the slip from me and put it on the bed with the other clothes we were taking to the mortician. His hands lingered on the soft material for a moment, then he slammed the drawer shut and turned to me. *"Don't ever save anything for a special occasion. Every day you're alive is a special occasion."*

I remembered those words through the funeral and the days that followed when I helped him and my niece attend to all the sad chores that follow an unexpected death. I thought about them on the plane returning to California from the Midwestern town where my sister's family lives. I thought about all the things that she hadn't seen, or heard, or done. I thought about the things that she had done without realizing that they were special. I'm still thinking about his words, and they've changed my life. I'm reading more and dusting less. I'm sitting on the deck and admiring the view without fussing about the weeds in the garden. I'm spending more time with my family and friends and less time in committee meetings.

Whenever possible, life should be a pattern of experience to savor, not endure. I'm trying to recognize these moments now and cherish them. I'm not "saving" anything. We use our good china and crystal for every special event such as losing a pound, getting the sink unstopped, the first camellia blossom. I wear my good blazer to the market if I feel like it. My theory is if I look prosperous, I can shell out $28.49 for one small bag of groceries without wincing. I'm not saving my good perfume for special parties. Clerks in hardware stores and tellers in banks have noses that function as well as my party-going friends.

"Someday" and "one of these days" are losing their grip on my vocabulary. If it's worth seeing, or hearing, or doing, I want to see and hear and do it now. I'm not sure what my sister would have done had she known that she wouldn't be here for the tomorrow we all take for granted. I think she would have called family members and a few close friends. She might have called a few former friends to apologize and mend fences for past squabbles. I like to think she would have gone out for a Chinese dinner, her favorite food. I'm guessing. I'll never know.

It's those little things left undone that would make me angry if I knew that my hours were limited. Angry because I put off seeing good friends whom I was going to get in touch with... someday. Angry because I hadn't written certain letters that I intended to write... one of these days. Angry and sorry that I didn't tell my husband and daughter often enough how much I truly love them.

I'm trying very hard not to put off, hold back, or save anything that would add laughter and luster to our lives. And every morning when I open my eyes, I tell myself that it is special. Every day, every minute, every breath truly is... a gift from God. (By Ann Wells...Los Angeles Times)

"Heavenly Father, life is a gift. You are Life and the greatest Gift of all. Thanks for all the special things You put into my life every second... every minute... every hour... every day. Forgive me for passing them by and postponing living until my life is in order. My life will never be 'in order' because we live in a fallen world. Your grace and goodness not only

make this journey bearable, but enjoyable. As a father myself, it blesses my heart to see my children enjoying my company and the little things I give them and do for them. Since You are the Ultimate Father, I know that You are blessed by my enjoying You and all the things you give me. Thanks, Daddy God. I love you. Amen."

3

And why worry about a speck in your friend's eye when you have a log in your own? —Matthew 7:3 NLT

I remember reading about a woman who purchased a magazine, a cup of coffee and a package of cookies at an airport canteen. She sat down at a table along with a man reading a newspaper. As she read her magazine, she reached for her cookies on the table and was shocked as the man took one of her cookies and began eating it. She glared at him while he continued to munch and smile at her. She was flabbergasted. She continued to read but couldn't keep her mind on the article. As she reached for another cookie, the man took a second one. Now she was upset. As she was about to boil over, the man took the last cookie, broke it in two and handed her the other half. She stuffed it in her mouth and stomped off down the concourse. As she poked her magazine into her pocketbook, she felt something. Upon inspection, she pulled out her package of cookies... unopened.

I'm a recovering Pharisee. At times, I'm a full-fledged Pharisee. I condemn and criticize people for their sins when, in fact, I'm more rotten and sinful than they are. I just don't like to admit it. This story hit me between the eyes. I want to help people get the speck out of their eyes when I have a log in my own. Jesus admonishes us to get the log out of our own eye, and then we will be able to help our brothers and sisters with the specks in theirs.

Every one of us without exception is self-centered and selfish. If we were honest, we really don't care that much about others except for how their attitudes and actions affect us. We are like the woman getting ticked off about the man eating what she thought were *her* cookies when in reality she was eating his. Wonder if he felt the same way she did? Evidently not. He was seemingly glad to share his cookies without her even asking while she was ready to smack him for doing the same thing.

Beloved, we are all in the same boat. We are fallen human beings living in a fallen, sinful world. Apart from the grace of God, we are capable of committing every evil act under the sun. Don't you agree? If you do agree, then why do we persist in looking down our spiritual noses at others? The ground is level at the cross. We all deserve death and hell no matter how self-righteous we think we are. Why don't we do what the Lord requires of us? What does the Lord require? You will find it in Micah 6:8, **"The LORD has already told you what is good, and this is what He requires: to do what is right, to love mercy, and to walk humbly with your God."** In other words, do what God says is right according to His Word. To love mercy means that we cut others some slack when they don't always do what is right. To walk humbly with the Lord means that when we do mess up, we admit it to Him and get back to doing what is right. That's all that the Lord requires of us.

We need to stop trying to pick specks out of other people's eyes and cookies out of their teeth. Admit that we desperately need a Savior and that our best is just not good enough. Isaiah said that **"we are all infected and impure with sin. When we proudly display our righteous deeds, we find they are but filthy rags"** (Isaiah 64:6 NLT). By the way, those rags to which he refers are menstrual rags. Is that a sickening thought, or what? We need Jesus really bad. We need to beg for His mercy and quit demanding justice. Had you rather have justice, or mercy? That's what I thought. Enjoy your cookies and share with one another... gladly.

"Heavenly Father, would You help me with this log in my eye? It's blinding me to how desperately I need You. Forgive me for poking other people in the eye by trying to fix them. I can't fix them. I can't even fix me. Would you fix me? Help me to do right, love mercy and walk humbly with You today. Thanks. Amen."

4

And then I will declare to them, "I never knew you."
—Matthew 7:23

How well do you think you know God? Have you settled for knowing less about God than He wants you to know? Do the following words penned by Wilbur Reese describe you?

> *"I would like to buy three dollars worth of God, please. Not enough to explode my soul or disturb my sleep, but just enough of Him to equal a cup of warm milk or a snooze in the sunshine. I don't want enough of Him to make me love a black man or pick beets with a migrant. I want ecstasy, not transformation. I want the warmth of the womb, not a new birth. I want a pound of the Eternal in a paper sack. I would like to buy three dollars worth of God, please."*

The Church, the body of true believers, is only as great as its concept of God. If you sense that your Christian experience is not what it should be, your problem is that you are not taking time to cultivate your relationship with the God who gave you life.

Jesus... My Final Answer

After Elvis Presley died, newspapers told of people who had almost made him god of their lives. One young man in Florida actually had plastic surgery to alter his face to look like Elvis. *"Presley has been my idol since I was five years old,"* he said. *"I have every record he has cut twice over, pictures by the thousands, even two leaves from a tree from the mansion in Memphis..."* But the tragic words of his interview fell flat as he confessed at the end, *"I never got close to him. I never saw him. I never knew him."*

I wonder if you and I will stand before God on the Day of Judgment and confess: *"I represented You, but I never got close to You. I never knew You deeply. I was busy about the work of Christianity without getting to know the Father of it all."*

How intimately do you know God? What does John 14:21 tell you about what you can do to experience God daily? **"Those who obey My commandments are the ones who love Me. And because they love Me, My Father will love them, and I will love them. And I will reveal Myself to each one of them"** (John 14:21 NLT). Christ demonstrated His love for us in that while we were still sinners, He died for us (Romans 5:8). We demonstrate our love for Him through total obedience and absolute, unconditional surrender to His Lordship. If you love Him enough to do that, He will become more real to you than you could ever imagine.

"Father God, please help me to see You at work around me every minute of everyday. Make me acutely aware that everything that touches my life has two purposes: Your glory and my benefit. That awareness alone is enough to fill my heart with thanksgiving and joy. Help me to always be responsive to Your slightest touch. I live to worship You. I ask You so many times to bless me. Today, may I be a blessing to You. Thanks for Your never-ending love for me. I love You, too. Amen."

5

Calling the Twelve to Him, He sent them out two by two and gave them authority over evil spirits. —Mark 6:7 NIV

What we read, what we watch on television, and the people we hang around with today will determine the person we become tomorrow. We become whatever we focus on, or identify with. We only identify with people that will accept us, love us, and are going in the same direction we are. We don't hang around people who don't like us, or care about us. Birds of a feather do flock together.

I have heard it said that the person who influences us the most is the person whom we believe in the most. I've changed my thinking on that. I believe that the person who influences us the most is the one who believes in us. Dr. Loyd Melton, my seminary Greek and New Testament professor, had a major influence upon my life. He could stand there and talk about the New Testament and make you feel like you were there. He could talk about what was going through the mind of the disciples as they tried to figure out that mysteriously wonderful Messiah. He could take you inside their minds and make you realize that they had the same thoughts that you and I have. I identified with him. I longed to please him... to make good grades... to make him proud. You know why? Because he believed in me.

Jesus... My Final Answer

I'll never forget what he wrote at the bottom of my last test paper before I left to move to North Carolina and another seminary. He wrote, *"Kenny, I have always sensed a very deep call of God upon your life. Don't be afraid. Wherever you go, He will lead the way. And on your journey, you will find Him waiting around every curve of the road. Teaching you has been a pleasure that others need to enjoy as I have. God bless you."*

There have been times in my life that were so dark I doubted my salvation not to mention my calling. But during those times, the Holy Spirit would bring to mind what Dr. Melton wrote on the bottom of that test. I would, like David, encourage myself in the Lord. *"Dr. Melton believed in me. If he believed in me and saw the calling then who am I to let him and the Lord down. I'm not going to cave in. I'm not going to doubt in the darkness what God has shown me in the light."*

I remember hearing a story one time about President Thomas Jefferson who was out riding horses with some friends. They came to a river that was swollen by great rains that had washed away the bridge. Crossing would be dangerous, but it was the only way to reach their destination. One by one they coaxed their horses into the raging waters and slowly made their way across. A stranger on foot was standing nearby watching to see how well they made it. Having witnessed their success, the stranger asked President Jefferson if he would give him a ride across the river. The President forded the river once again and carried the stranger across.

As they reached the other side, one of the men asked the stranger, *"Do you realize that you asked the President of the United States to carry you across the river?"*

"No, I did not know that?" he replied.

"What made you ask him instead of one of us?" the man asked.

Jesus... My Final Answer

The stranger said, *"He had a 'YES' face. The rest of you had a 'NO' face."*

People with "YES" faces encourage us to ask... to reach... to climb... to be all we can be because they treat us as if we are worthy of the time and effort they put into us. Jesus had the greatest "YES" face of all. That's why He was a friend of sinners, and why religious people hated Him. Religious people who think you have to pull your own weight to be worthy of grace all wear "NO" faces. That's why sinners don't come to churches run by legalists and rule-keepers.

Let me ask you something. Do you have a "YES" face? Are people drawn to you because you respect, trust and honor them as a precious creation made in the image of God? Jesus trusted His disciples with His own authority. He sent them out to preach the gospel, cast out demons and heal people in His Name. And they were far from being perfect. One was a thief. One denied he ever knew Him. Two wanted places of honor for themselves. But He still believed in them. He still trusted them to act on His behalf. And He still believes in you.

How long are you going to cower in fear on the banks of the raging river that separates you from your destination afraid to ask for a ride? God always keeps His promises. He tells us to ask Him. Don't be afraid. Just ask. **"For no matter how many promises God has made, they are all "Yes" in Christ"** (2 Corinthians 1:20 NIV). Jesus never takes His "YES" face off. You have not because you ask not. Go for it, Beloved!

"Heavenly Father, thank You for believing in me. You trusted me so much that You sent Your Son to die for me while I was still a sinner. If You believed in me that much, and I've given You reasons not to, why do I not trust in You when You have never given me reason to doubt You? Forgive me, Father. Thanks for believing in me. I think I'm going to make it. Give

me grace to keep my 'YES' face on for everyone I meet today. Feel free to ask me to do anything You need me to do for You today. I've always got my 'YES' face on for You. Amen."

6

"I tell you the truth, anyone who will not receive the kingdom of God like a little child will never enter it."
—Mark 10:15 NIV

I have a good friend named Matthew. He is 17 years old and a very special young man. Matthew has Down's Syndrome, but it doesn't bother Matthew one bit. He is one of the best Christian young men I know. He is polite, respectful, well-mannered, responsible and the most loving 17 year old I know. He is great. I love him.

Today, we took our weekly trip to McDonald's. If there is anything that Matthew likes better than eating, I don't know what it could be. We get the same thing every week. Matthew gets two fish sandwiches, an order of fries, tea and an apple pie. Every week. Week in and week out. The cashier doesn't even have to ask for our order anymore. She knows. We love our time together at McDonald's.

On the way to lunch, I told Matthew that we needed to pray for some rain. At the time, we were experiencing a severe drought of several weeks. Matthew said, *"Okay. Father, we need some rain really, really bad. The plants are thirsty, and they will die if they don't have any rain. Father, will you please send us some rain. Thank You. Amen."*

Jesus... My Final Answer

Immediately our verse for today came to mind. Matthew lives in the Kingdom. As a matter of fact, he never leaves. He knows Father has whatever he or anyone else needs. He knows how to ask and is not ashamed to do so. He is free to love and enjoy life. He is absolutely fearless and is honest without offense.

A couple of friends came by our table to talk while we were eating. I introduced Matthew. Matthew said, *"My name is Matthew. And yours?"*

Our friend said, *"My name is Jeff, Matthew."*

"It's nice to meet you, Jeff," Matthew politely replied.

Matthew has no hang-ups. He doesn't worry about what people think about him. He loves life, people and fish sandwiches... maybe not in that order. You'll have to ask Matthew. He just believes God is good and can do anything. Matthew says you just have to ask Him.

Matthew comes to our Sunday night men's prayer meeting. He prays as well and as often as any man there. And when Matthew prays, you just know Father is listening. Why? Because Matthew trusts Him. Matthew is not afraid to ask God anything. He knows that Father loves him and everyone else. There are no prisons for Matthew. He is free because Jesus set him free.

Maybe we are a little too "grown up" to pray. Maybe we are afraid to come out of our prisons and walk in the freedom that Christ died to give us. Maybe if we just took Christ at His Word... Maybe if we started acting like children... You never know. Matthew says it works for him. Jesus says it will work for you, too. Why don't you give it a whirl today?

By the way, it rained that afternoon for the first time in two months!

"Heavenly Father, I don't live and enjoy life like a child. You tell me that if I don't start, then I won't ever enter Your Kingdom. You have opened the door to my cage, but I have to

get off my perch and fly out. You won't reach in and drag me out. I have to choose. Today, give me the grace and courage to live with reckless abandon like a little child. I'm tired of mediocrity and a "ho-hum" existence. I want to live... really live. Let's have some fun today, Father. This is the day that You have made. I will rejoice and be glad in it. Amen."

7

I tell you the truth, anyone who will not receive the kingdom of God like a little child will never enter it.
—Luke 18:17 NIV

Prayer is simply telling God to do what He already wants to do. He will not do what He wants to do until we tell Him to do it. Sound crazy? God said it Himself. ***Thus says the LORD, The Holy One of Israel, and his Maker: "Ask Me of things to come concerning My sons; and concerning the work of My hands, YOU COMMAND ME"*** (Isaiah 45:11 NKJV). Is that amazing or what!?! God wants to be glorified on earth. That's a fancy name for letting people see Who He really is and what He's like. God knows if people see Him the way He really is, they would most definitely accept and worship Him as Lord and Savior.

God desires our help. Oh, He could do it Himself, but He likes having us cooperate with Him in getting His way done down here on earth. The way we help is by praying. It goes like this: God has things He wants to do which we call "His will." He sends the Holy Spirit to show us what He wants to do. We then tell God to do what He wants to do which is what God calls prayer. When we pray and tell God to do what He wants to do, He does it, and people see what a great God He is. Everybody's happy, the devil gets his teeth kicked, and God is glorified as His will is done on earth as it is in heaven. Can it get any simpler?

Then what's the problem. I found out Sunday morning while I was preaching. I was explaining this very simplistic yet profound concept of prayer to my beloved congregation. The Lord gave me this great illustration. After explaining how God promised to give us blessing upon blessing if we would only ask, I took out the candy jar I keep on my desk. I held it up and declared: *"It is my will to give you this candy."* Everybody sat there like a knot on a log. I repeated: *"It is my will to give anyone who asks and comes forward to receive it, all the candy you want."* You know who came, don't you? I was flooded with kids from all corners of the church. A few adults who, bless God, have not lost their childlike love of life came as well. The last one to come was a little girl about two feet tall who came all the way from the back. She reached her little hand in that jar and pulled out a handful of candy that Goliath couldn't have handled. It blessed my heart to no end.

As I watched her dig deep into the jar, the Holy Spirit gently whispered, **"Those who won't come and receive like this little girl will not enter the Kingdom of God."** How sad that we have become too sophisticated to take God at His Word. Those kids came running, knocking each other out of the way. They were unashamed. All they knew was that candy was available if they could just get to the front of the church to get it. Nothing else mattered to them at the time. Our problem is that too much matters to us "big people" all the time. God has His hand on the lever just dying to open the flood gates of heaven, and we are too proper to holler at Him to pull it.

That reminds me of a story I heard one time. It seems as if one man died and went to heaven to be greeted by the Lord Jesus. As the Lord gave Him the grand tour, the man was utterly amazed at the glory of the Lord and the beauty of heaven. Finally, they came to this large room filled with the most beautifully wrapped packages... all shapes, sizes and colors. The man asked the Lord to explain. The Lord replied, **"My son, all these blessings were yours, but you were too occupied with other matters to ask for them."**

"Heavenly Father, forgive me for acting like a prudish grown-up when it comes to Kingdom matters. Only children, and we are all children in Your eyes, will ever enter the Kingdom and help You make Your Kingdom come and Your will be done on earth as it is in heaven. You want me to have childlike faith. Lord give it to me. I want it. I receive it. Thank you, Lord. Give me bigger spiritual hands and a longer reach so that I can dig deeper into Your candy jar of grace and blessing. Tell me what You want to do, and I'll be glad to tell You to do it. Let me and all of us down here see what a great God you are. Let me be a blessing to You today. You command me. Amen."

8

But if you are unwilling to serve the LORD, then choose today whom you will serve... But as for me and my family, we will serve the LORD." —Joshua 24:15 NLT

I woke up early today, excited over all God and I get to do before the clock strikes midnight. He has given me responsibilities to fulfill today. God thinks I am important. My job is to choose what kind of day we are going to have.

    Today I can complain because the weather is rainy, or I can be thankful that the grass is getting watered for free.

    Today I can feel sad that I don't have more money, or I can be glad that my finances encourage me to plan my purchases wisely and guide me away from waste.

    Today I can grumble about my health, or I can rejoice that I am alive.

    Today I can lament over all that my parents didn't give me when I was growing up, or I can feel grateful that they allowed me to be born.

    Today I can cry because roses have thorns, or I can celebrate that thorns have roses.

    Today I can mourn my lack of friends, or I can excitedly embark upon a quest to discover new relationships.

Today I can whine because I have to go to work, or I can shout for joy because I have a job to do. I can complain because I have to go to school or eagerly open my mind and fill it with rich new tidbits of knowledge.

Today I can murmur dejectedly because I have to do housework, or I can feel honored because the Lord has provided shelter for my mind, body and soul.

Today stretches ahead of me, waiting to be shaped. I can stay on God's pottery wheel and let Him mold me into a vessel unto honor, or I can choose to jump off and reside in the darkness of the clay bin. God lets me choose what kind of day I will have!

Today is like a dollar. You only get to spend it once. Make sure God gets His money's worth. Choose wisely.

"Heavenly Father, thank You for Life in Christ. The day that I surrendered my heart to You, I started living on borrowed time... Your time. I live for one purpose and one purpose only... to love and worship You with all my heart, mind, soul and strength. I choose Life today. I choose Grace today. I choose the road less traveled. I choose the straight and narrow gate. I thank You that You have given me the choice because You chose me before the foundation of the world (Ephesians 1:4). May the choices I make lead others to choose You as well. Amen."

9

And Jesus said to her, "Neither do I condemn you; go and sin no more." —John 8:11 NKJV

A lady walked into a Hallmark Card Shop. A clerk came up and asked if she could be of assistance. The lady replied, *"Yes. I need a get-well card with a hint of I-told-you-so."* There's just something in our fleshly nature that just loves to be right. Not only do we love to be right, we also love to flaunt it in the face of those "less right" than we are. Oh, how we love to gloat.

Our verse today comes from the story of the woman caught in adultery. A group of religious people who were always right had caught her in the very act of adultery. The Law said that she was to be put to death... or at least that was their interpretation. **"If a man commits adultery with another man's wife, both the man and the woman must be put to death"** (Leviticus 20:10 NLT). My question has always been: Where was the man? I thought it took two to commit adultery. Were these religious people committed to keeping the purity of the Law, or were they out to entrap Jesus?

Jesus never ceases to amaze me. The religious establishment was constantly trying to put Jesus between a rock and a hard place. They asked questions that could not be answered by human wisdom without causing division. Jesus always found a way to proclaim truth in a way that gave hope to sinners and completely shut the mouths of the self-righteous. In this instance, some people think that Jesus threw the Law out the window when He let the woman go free, but that's not the case. *"On the testimony of two or three witnesses a man shall be put to death, but no one shall be put to death on the testimony of only one witness. The hands of the witnesses must be the first in putting him to death"* (Deuteronomy 17:6-7 NIV).

Jesus addressed the crowd, **"Okay, go ahead and stone her. But let he who has never sinned throw the first stone."** One by one, beginning with the oldest, they turned and walked away. When there was no one left, Jesus asked the woman, **"Woman, where are your accusers? Is there no one here to condemn you?"**

"No, Lord," she replied.

"Then neither do I condemn you. Go and sin no more."

Had there been two witnesses that could have verified the truth, Jesus would have allowed them to stone her. But there were no witnesses. Jesus knew she was an adulteress. The woman knew she was an adulteress. Jesus also knew she was sick of living in sin and in desperate need hope. That's why He didn't condemn her. She would have been more than willing to turn from her sin had she something, or someone, to turn to.

It's remarkable that Jesus was right and she was wrong, and yet He didn't give her the old "I-told-you-so" speech. Let me tell you something right now. Jesus is on your side. He's not against you. He's for you. You can come to Him anytime no matter how filthy and sinful you are. He will not condemn you, chide you, or lecture you. He's not out to get you. He wants you to come let Him forgive you, heal your wounds and meet your unmet needs that caused you to sin

Jesus... My Final Answer

in the first place. His invitation to come and get well comes with no "I-told-you-so's."

Now there, I told you so. He's waiting for You.

"Heavenly Father, I, too, love to be right. I especially love to tell all the know-it-all's how right I am when they are wrong. Thank You that You are not that way. You are always right. I am the one who is wrong. I'm only right when I'm in agreement with You. I hate to admit it, but I'm not always as loving, forgiving and gracious as You. Bless You for giving me mercy instead of justice. May I have Your grace to extend the same courtesy to others today? Amen."

10

For the sinful nature desires what is contrary to the Spirit, and the Spirit what is contrary to the sinful nature. They are in conflict with each other, so that you do not do what you want. —Gal 5:16-17 NIV

I have been playing golf for over thirty-five years. I love it although it is the most humbling and frustrating game in the world. The reason that the game is so aggravating is because the conventional way to play golf is totally opposite to the way you would naturally try to swing the club. It's like walking in the Spirit and walking in the flesh. Both are contrary to one another. An old evangelist used to say, *"If it feels natural, it ain't spiritual."*

Golf is a crazy game. If you want the ball to go to the right, you swing to the left. If you want it to go left, you swing to the right. If you want it to go up in the air, you swing down. If you want it to go low, you swing up. How unnatural is that?

Back in the mid 1980's, a physicist set out to find the most efficient way to swing a golf club. After much research and development, he came up with a method that became known as Natural Golf (NG for short). It was named Natural Golf because the swing was made the way you would naturally want to swing the golf club. Note the differences between

NG and Conventional Golf (CG for short): In NG, you hold the club in the palm. In CG, the fingers. In NG, you restrict your hip and shoulder turn on the backswing. In CG, you are taught to make big shoulder and hip turns. In NG, the planes of the arms and club are on the same plane. In CG, there are two planes. Both methods are entirely in opposition to one another.

I played golf by the conventional method for thirty-five years. My swing was well ingrained with CG. With CG, if you are going to play well, you must practice a lot. Your muscles are called upon in CG to work in ways they are not accustomed to working. They must be trained constantly through muscle memory, or your swing will deteriorate. With NG, on the other hand, the muscles get to act "naturally." They don't have to go against the grain, so to speak.

About a year ago, I decided to convert my swing to Natural Golf because I do not get to practice very much. With CG, if you don't practice, you don't play well. Golf, for me, is not fun unless I play well. At first, the NG swing felt really weird. My mind was filled with all those CG swing thoughts from thirty-five years of practice. I hit some awful looking shots when I first started NG. As a matter of fact, I shot some terrible scores with my NG swing. Talk about frustrating. My conventional swing was not good enough for me to continue using it, and the natural swing was killing me because I couldn't get the old thought patterns and muscle memory out of my mind. I was playing so badly that a friend of mine gave me a suggestion. *"Kenny, I think you ought to take two weeks off from playing and practicing to clear your mind. Then after that, if I were you, I'd quit playing golf altogether."* Talk about Job's friends...

It's been a year now since I converted to NG. Everyday it becomes a little more natural. It feels like the way you're supposed to swing the golf club. When I swing the club naturally, the ball just takes off straight and long with an effortlessness that is absolutely wonderful. The only time I hit the ball badly is when some conventional part of the swing raises it ugly head during my natural swing. The two swings are mutually exclusive. When you mix the two, you get a mess, and the ball goes no where near the target.

There are so many parallels between these two golf swings and the war that the Spirit and flesh wage within us. Walking in the Spirit is the Super-Natural way to live. ***"If any man be in Christ, he is a new creation. Old things have passed away. Behold, all things have become new"*** (2 Corinthians 5:17). When we are born again, Christ becomes our life. We had no life before Jesus gave us His life. We were dead in trespasses and sins. Our new Spirit life is the way God naturally intended for us to live before the Fall of creation. After the Fall, man began to learn the conventional method of living... independently, soulishly, selfishly, fleshly. We tried to meet our own needs in our own energy rather than relying upon God and His provisions for us.

We experience the same frustration trying to live the Christian life as we do when we try to convert from CG to NG. Walking in the Spirit is so effortless and tireless, but the flesh wants to get into the act. Walking in the Spirit, allowing Jesus to live in and through us, is so natural. We just have to give up control and let Him swing us the way He desires. But we have been trained by the flesh for so long; our fleshly thoughts and actions are pretty well ingrained. Whenever we mix the two, it's really ugly. How can you be selfless and selfish at the same time? Pretty difficult, isn't it?

After a year of playing golf naturally, I don't think I could go back to playing conventionally. Yes, I've been frustrated, but I'm convinced that NG is a better way to play. For me, I'm convinced that it is the ONLY way to play. I'm also convinced that walking in the Spirit is the way to live my life with meaning, purpose and joy. However, when I get stressed out, I am tempted to revert back to my old, fleshly way of coping with problems. That is when life becomes a mess.

When I first started NG, I hit some really bad shots, but I didn't give up. When I first started walking in the Spirit, my flesh aggravated me to death and prevented me from glorifying Christ and living in His peace. But I did not, and I will not give up. Now, before I get out of bed each morning, I give control of my life to Jesus. I ask Him for grace to deny the flesh and submit to His Spirit. He is constantly renewing my mind so that my swing thoughts during the day are becoming His. As I take on the mind of Christ, I do what He NATURALLY wants me to do. Oh, how effortless and joyous life becomes when we allow His power, His grace and His life to flow through us.

"Therefore, my dear brothers and sisters, stand firm. Let nothing move you. Always give yourselves fully to the work of the Lord, because you know that your labor in the Lord is not in vain" (1 Corinthians 15:58).

"Dear Lord, thank You for saving me and making me Your child. I want to live today the way You naturally want me to live... in joy, peace, love and harmony with You and with my fellow man. Grant me the grace to honor and glorify You so that others will see that You are the Super-Natural way to live. Today, Lord, nothing but fairways and greens. Amen."

11

Then Jacob woke up and said, "Surely the LORD is in this place, and I wasn't even aware of it." —Genesis 28:16 NLT

I don't know about you, but there have been times in my life when I felt like my prayers never even reached the ceiling, and God was no where to be found. Then years later, I would look back at those times and see that God was not only there, but He was in total control.

I was twenty-eight years old when God woke me up. I had been saved since I was twelve, but I had no awareness of a relationship with Him. Christianity for me up to that point was doing what was right and hoping you didn't tick God off in the meantime. Even though I was unaware of His presence, He was still as close as the mention of His Name. One fateful night in August, 1977, the Lord set me on a journey that is still in progress. I was teaching and coaching high school, and the Lord asked me to start a chapter of The Fellowship of Christian Athletes. That year we started out with thirty kids meeting regularly for Bible study, morning devotions and bonfires. Five years later, we had over two hundred kids involved many of whom are in full-time Christian service today. God used the FCA to launch me into the pastorate and the gospel ministry. But my goodness, how close I came to missing Him completely.

Jesus... My Final Answer

I married my high school sweetheart when I was twenty years old. I believe marriage is the second most important decision you will ever make, and I never prayed about marrying Wanda. I was in love, and she was the only thing on my mind. Even though I didn't consult Him about the decision, my Bride was the one the Lord had chosen to complete me. She is my best friend, my lover and the best gift outside of Himself that He has ever given me. He was orchestrating His plan for us, and I wasn't even aware of it.

After we were married, we built a house and never consulted the Lord about it. But as always, He was working things out behind the scenes. A few years later, I let some disgruntled coaches talk me into leaving education and finding a real job making some real money. I never prayed about that decision either. I left my teaching/coaching job and took a job as an industrial engineer in a textile plant. I lasted one week. I would get sick every time I walked into work. God was there gently prodding me back into my destiny, and I wasn't even aware of it.

I resigned from that job on Monday, July 7, 1975 without even having another job. What was I thinking? All I knew was that I could not work another day in that mill, or I would have died. For some odd reason, I decided to stop by the high school on my way home. Mr. Monts, the principal, was out in the front yard. He greeted me kindly and asked, *"How's the new job, Coach?"*

"Mr. Monts, I just resigned," I sheepishly replied. *"I just didn't fit there. You don't happen to know of any teaching jobs open in the district, do you?"*

"It's strange that you ask. We haven't filled your job yet. Do you want it back?" he asked.

"Is the Pope Catholic? Do bears run naked through the woods? Is a pig pork? You better believe I want it back. Where do I sign?"

There are times in your life when things happen, and you just can't explain it other than, "God did it." It was a "God thing." We are talking about the middle of July with football practice starting in three weeks, and God kept His job for me open. Good coaching jobs are as scarce as hen's teeth, and mine was still available even at such a late date. I couldn't believe it. God was keeping me on track, and I wasn't even aware of it. Two years later, I would begin the FCA and the journey would continue.

I could spend the rest of this book telling about times when God was working, and I wasn't even aware of it. I'm sure you could, too. My point for all this "unawareness" is not to give you a license for slackness and prayerlessness. It's to show you how great and wonderful and wise and loving and good God really is. He does, indeed, take care of those who can't take care of themselves. That pretty much includes all of us, doesn't it? When I think of the times I've done something stupid, and God bailed me out...

Beloved, He loves you so much. He never slumbers nor sleeps, but watches over you 24/7 (Psalm 121:4). You are the apple of His eye. He knows the plans He has for you. Plans to prosper you and not harm you. Plans to give you a future and a hope (Jeremiah 29:11). Trust Him... even when you don't sense His presence. Believe me, He is there. If you take time to look back over your life, I'm sure you will see His fingerprints all over the place... even when you weren't aware of it. Especially, when you weren't aware of it. The Lord is working all things together for our good... even the bad times. I just wanted to make you aware that He is never unaware.

"Heavenly Father, I'm at a loss for words. I don't have it in me to thank You adequately for loving me the way You do. Make me more aware of Your greatness and majesty today. Amen."

12

As far as I am concerned, God turned into good what you meant for evil. —Genesis 50:20 NLT

On October 8, 1871, the Great Chicago Fire swept through the Windy City leaving 300 people dead, 100,000 homeless and 18,000 buildings destroyed. The estimated damage was a whopping $200 million... in 1871! The story goes that Mrs. O'Leary's cow, Daisy, started it all by kicking over a lantern in the barn even though Mrs. O'Leary denies even having a lantern.

Regardless of how the great fire started, it did. In the aftermath, the people of Chicago had to choose how they would respond to the tragedy. They could pout, complain and have a pity party, or they could role up their sleeves and get to work. Chicago responded positively. First of all, National Fire Prevention Week was created which has prevented numerous similar tragedies of which we will never know about on this side of heaven. Secondly, the Chicago Fire Department Training Academy now sits on what was once Mrs. O'Leary's and Daisy's barn.

Beloved, the Bible says that *"people are born for trouble as predictably as sparks fly upward from a fire"* (Job 5:7 NLT). Jesus said, **"In the world, you shall have tribulation"** (John 16:33). We need to understand in light of these verses that God is more concerned with our *response* to what is happening to us than He is about *what* is happening to us. We have a choice. We get to choose our attitude. We can have the mind of Christ, or the mind of the world, the flesh or the devil. We are going to have trials, difficulties and problems. It is our decision as to whether those things become stumbling blocks, or stepping stones. Our attitude determines whether the bumps in life are what we climb on, or what trips us up. That reminds me of one of my favorite poems.

> *Isn't is strange that princes and kings, and clowns that caper in sawdust rings,*
> *And common people like you and me are builders of our destiny.*
> *Each is given a bag of tools, some building blocks and a Book of rules.*
> *And each must make e're life is flown, as stumbling block, or a stepping stone.* (Author Unknown)

Joseph had the right attitude when he was reunited with his brothers who had sold him into slavery down in Egypt. **"God meant for good what you meant for evil"** (Genesis 50:20). God works all things together for our good if we love Him and are called according to His purpose (Romans 8:28). God knows what we need in order to fulfill our destiny. He supplies the building blocks and the raw material. Use what God supplies for you to work with today and keep your tools sharp and ready. And don't forget to follow the Directions.

"Heavenly Father, I acknowledge that You are the Master Builder and Architect of my life. I'm just the construction worker. I work with what You supply. Sometimes I second guess the materials You give me to work with. Forgive me when I try

to take over Your job. Thanks in advance for whatever You order up for me today. Thanks for the tools You've given me. May I use them wisely and well for Your glory. Amen."

13

*Truly you are a God who hides Himself,
O God and Savior of Israel.* —Isaiah 45:15 NIV

We live in a society that accentuates feelings and warm fuzzies. We adhere to the philosophy that seeing is believing. Our soul longs to feel God... to touch Him... to see His face. What soul wouldn't? But God is a God Who, indeed, hides Himself. He is so beyond our comprehension. It has been said that when a worm can comprehend the complexities of man, then man will be able to understand all there is to know about God.

We have all experienced times when the heavens turn to brass, and God feels a million light years away. And if you have been in religious circles for very long, you have probably been made to feel that you were "unspiritual," or that the sin in your life was stifling His manifest presence. If you are experiencing His "hiddenness," I'm here to tell you that God is not mad at you, nor disappointed in you. If I'm not mistaken, God poured out His wrath for my sins and yours upon Jesus on the Cross. He paid for our sins, and we are no longer enemies of God. *"Surely He took up our infirmities and carried our sorrows, yet we considered Him stricken by God, smitten by Him, and afflicted. But He was pierced for our transgressions, He was crushed for our iniquities; the punishment that brought us peace was upon Him, and by His wounds we are healed"* (Isaiah 53:4-5 NIV). Jesus took all our punishment. We have none coming to us anymore. How good is that?

God's hiddenness is not a sign of His disapproval but of His pleasure. *When all the people were being baptized, Jesus was baptized too. And as He was praying, heaven was opened and the Holy Spirit descended on Him in bodily form like a dove. And a voice came from heaven:* "**You are my Son, Whom I love; with You I am well pleased**" (Luke 3:21-22 NIV). Father God was well pleased with His Son and told Him so as John baptized Him in the Jordan River. But look what happened next. *"Jesus, full of the Holy Spirit, returned from the Jordan and was led by the Spirit in the desert, where for forty days He was tempted by the devil"* (Luke 4:1-2 NIV).

Note Who it was that led Him into the wilderness where Father hid from Him. It was the Holy Spirit. Why did Father do that to the Son He loved? Because He was preparing His Son for the sprint to the Cross. Father knew that Jesus would be pushed to the limits of His soul and all vestiges of His soul had to be weaned away. After all, the Word says that Jesus learned obedience through the things that He suffered (Hebrews 5:8). Although He was 100% God, He was also 100% Man with a soul like ours which likes to have God on its own terms. His soul desires had to be dealt with before He could fulfill His destiny as our Redeemer. As Watchman Nee says, God was weaning Jesus off His soul. God had a divine purpose in allowing Jesus to experience the wilderness. He returned to Galilee in the power of the Spirit (Luke 4:14). Soulish desires rob us of His power and strength. They have to go.

Faith is seeing with spiritual eyes rather than physical eyes. That is why God sometimes hides Himself from us. He put us in a room and says, **"I will never leave you, nor**

forsake You." Then He cuts off the lights. It becomes so dark in our soul that we can't see our proverbial hand in front of our face. All we have is His promise that He is still as close as He ever was when we walked in His manifest presence. He whispers, **"Don't doubt in the darkness what I have shown you in the light."**

Of course, this time of hiddenness is a prime time for the enemy of our souls to taunt us, *"Where is this loving God of yours now? Why He is so disappointed in you that He's left you high and dry? When are you going to wise up and forget about Him?"* As he accuses, Father God hides and Jesus prays that our faith won't fail. It's a time to purge our soulishness for our sprint to the Cross and our destiny in Christ.

God's hiddenness is a time in which He is trying to give us deeper Truth than we've ever known before. We are unable to comprehend deep Truth when we are in His manifest presence. Don't you remember how the disciples never understood what Jesus was talking about when He told them that He was going to Jerusalem to die? Why didn't they understand? It was because Jesus' presence is very distracting. When we're experiencing His presence, all we can think about is how wonderful it is to be with Him. That is why He has to hide Himself from time to time in order to implant deep Truth into us for future ministry. Even John the Baptist wondered if Jesus was the One during his time of God's hiddenness. And remember that John heard God Himself proclaim that Jesus was the One right before his very eyes.

So, Beloved, if God is nowhere to be found, and you are wallowing in self-pity, get up. Dust yourself off and rejoice. God has not forgotten about you. He is about to promote you to the front ranks of His army. He is trying to impart to you the keys of the Kingdom. What a blessing He is giving you. Don't be discouraged. Take heart. He is here. He hides so we will seek Him. And He promises that we will find Him if we search for Him with all our heart (Jeremiah 29:13).

Let's play hide-and-seek, Lord. You hide... I'll seek!

"Heavenly Father, all this time I thought Your were hiding from me because You were displeased with me. I'm so thankful that You trust me enough to impart deeper Truth into me. Lord, give me grace to keeping believing and walking in faith even when the way is dark and You are nowhere to be found. You hide and I'll seek. But You can let me find You whenever You please. Amen."

14

And so, after he (Abraham) had patiently endured, he obtained the promise. —Hebrews 6:15 NKJV

Consider the postage stamp. Its usefulness consists in its ability to stick to one thing until it gets there. It's a shame there are not more "postage stamp" Christians. It seems that *commitment* is an endangered species. People will tell you they will go to hell and back with you, and then when things heat up, they let you make the trip alone. Thank God for Jesus. He went to hell and back for us so we didn't have to go at all, much less alone. He is a Friend that "sticks" closer than a brother (Proverbs 17:17).

I'm sure you've heard the story about the pig and the chicken who happened by a church breakfast one day. The chicken said, *"Hey, let's drop in and make a contribution to the breakfast."* The pig replied, *"It may be a contribution for you, but it's total commitment for me."*

Did Jesus totally commit Himself to us for time and eternity? Was He, Who knew no sin, made sin for us? Did He leave Heaven's glory to come to earth to die in our place? How's that for total commitment? What does the word "Christian" mean anyway? Does it not mean "Christ-like"? Did we not realize when we made our commitment to Christ that we were called to follow in His steps (I Peter 2:21)? And we know where His steps led... up a hill called Calvary. If we follow Him, His steps will lead us up the same hill. Is He worth it?

Jesus said that He always did those things that pleased His Father (John 5:30). Do we always do those things that please Him? Did we not count the cost when we made our commitment to Him? Or did we put our hand to the plow and look back making us unfit for the Kingdom (Luke 9:62)?

God is a "crockpot." The world is a "microwave." The two are always at odds with one another. God never gets in a hurry. The world never slows down. God wants us to be patient. We want patience, and we want it NOW! Abraham received the promises of God because he patiently endured. The Greek word here is **makrothumeo**. **Makros** means "long." **Thumos** means "mind." The term means "to set your mind for the long haul."

Life is not a sprint. It's a marathon. Pinto beans taste so much better cooked in a crockpot rather than "nuked" in a microwave. It takes commitment to run the race and to enjoy gourmet pintos. If you are going to enter the race for the long haul, you better eat something that will "stick" to your ribs.

Keep a steady pace, Beloved. I'll see you at the finish line.

"Father, patience is not my long suit. Help me today to wait upon You and strengthen me for this leg of the race today. Amen."

15

There is really only one thing worth being concerned about. Mary has discovered it--and I won't take it away from her.
—Luke 10:42 NLT

～

The flesh can't rest. It has to be doing something. It hungers for approval... a way of measuring its worth and value. That is why the flesh loves the Law of God. It becomes frustrated that it cannot attain to the Law's perfection, but the Law makes a great measuring device for comparison to others. *"I read my Bible... I pray... I go to church... I do good deeds... I don't drink, cuss, smoke, or chew, or go with girls who do. I am good. Look what I do compared to you!"*

The flesh never understands that we are not who we are because of what we do. We do what we do because of Whose we are. Jesus has already done for us everything that ever needed doing. Because of His doing, we can simply rest in Him and allow Him to live in and through us. We don't stop doing, but our doing is in the power of the Spirit and not of the flesh.

God's people have always struggled with fleshly doing. **"God will speak to this people, 'This is the resting place, let the weary rest'; and, 'This is the place of repose'--*but they would not listen. So then, the Word of the LORD to them will become: Do and do, do and do, rule on rule, rule*** *on rule; a little here, a little there-- so that they will go and fall backward, be injured and snared and captured"* (Isaiah 28:11-13 NIV). Whenever we try to earn approval and acceptance via our performance, frustration and disappointment hound us every step of the way. Until we give up trying, we do and do to the point of exhaustion. Then we re-dedicate our lives to God and vow to do better next time. And then the cycle starts all over again. Some just give up and quit trying. Others are too stubborn to quit. Few discover the reality of entering into His rest.

In Luke chapter 10, we find Jesus paying a visit to the home of Martha and Mary, Lazarus' sisters. Martha is in the kitchen working herself into a dither trying to prepare a great meal for the Lord. Mary is in the living room sitting at His feet soaking in His presence. Martha is ticked off. *"Lord, tell Mary to get off her blessed assurance and get in here to help me. Who does she think she is?"* Jesus' answer goes right to the source of Martha's frustration. **"My dear Martha, you are so upset over all these details! There is really only one thing worth being concerned about. Mary has discovered it — and I won't take it away from her"** (Luke 10:41-42 NLT).

Did you notice how Jesus addressed Martha? **"Dear Martha..."** You can almost feel His love and acceptance of her even though she is 180 degrees off course. He still loves her and longs for her to end her frustration by simply doing the only thing that really matters... trusting and resting in Him and His love. Mary found that ONE thing and the Lord commended her. And she wasn't doing a thing.

Years ago when I really became serious about serving the Lord, I would constantly ask God what I could do for Him. If I was not doing something of eternal value like reading the Bible, or praying, or witnessing, I felt like the Lord was disappointed in me. The only time I ever felt any value was when I was doing something for the Lord. Then one day, the

Lord answered me. **"So, Kenny, you want to do something for Me. Okay, here is what I want you to do. Sit down and let's talk. I want to hang out with you, but you are so busy running around doing something FOR Me that you never have time to be WITH Me. Stay here with Me until leaving My presence to do something for Me is the last thing you want to do. Then you will be ready to do something."**

I'll have to admit that for a while, I felt like I was backslidden. I realized that I had become a "human doing," not a "human being." All the things I did because *I* thought the Lord wanted me to do them, I cut them out. The Lord began to pull off my grave clothes of legalism, perfectionism and fleshly doing. He's still working on me. I still feel the flesh raise up its ugly old head every now and then, but now I stop and rest in Him.

Looks like you could use a rest yourself. If you just have to DO something, run on over and jump in His lap. That's all you need to DO!

"Heavenly Father, the joy of the Lord is my strength. Sometimes I feel like all my strength is gone. Doing and doing and doing has taken its toll on me and robbed me of Your joy. I need Your grace now not to do something, but to stop doing those things that You never asked me to do. Is it okay if I just rest here with You awhile? Thanks, Lord, for all You've done! Amen."

16

Only I can tell you what is going to happen even before it happens. —Isaiah 46:9-10 NLT

Our verse for today sort of knocks all the psychics in the head, doesn't it? Only God can tell us what is going to happen. We all want to know what the future holds, don't we? That's why 900 numbers are flooding the market. But do we really want to know what the future holds? If you knew the world was coming to an end on January 1st, would you live any differently? Why would you change? The world could end for you, or someone you love today much less tomorrow, or months down the road. Are you doing the important things today? Are you loving your spouse and your kids? Are you telling them so? Are you treating people in a way that points them to Christ, or are you indifferent and apathetic? If you knew someone you dearly loved was going to die in a month, would it paralyze you with worry and dread and keep you from pursuing your destiny in Christ?

Maybe that's why God wants us to simply trust and obey Him minute by minute, hour by hour. Life by the yard gets pretty hard. Life by the inch is a cinch. God is too loving to ever hurt us to our detriment. He is too wise to ever make a mistake. And He is so powerful and sovereign that nothing can thwart His purposes. Do you believe that? Then why do we need to know the future? Could it be that we want to be in control rather than allowing God to be?

For instance, suppose that our government received a tip about the plans of the terrorists prior to 9/11. Suppose they implemented measures to prevent the attacks. Increased security and the subsequent delays at airports and large public gatherings would have been met with irate and vehement disapproval. Racial profiling of Middle Eastern men would have been met with outrage by the Civil Liberties Union. Americans would have perceived all of the post 9/11 measures as dangerous fanaticism and the backlash of criticism would have been phenomenal. Why? Because we would have never seen the tragedy and heartache that was prevented because God intervened and stopped it and remained anonymous.

Why are we so stubborn? God gets the blame all the time for bad stuff that happens, but He gets little or no credit for the innumerable bad things He prevents. A lot of the stuff that happens to us which we greet with irritation and frustration are simply things that God is orchestrating to prevent tragedy and heartache in our lives.

Josh McDowell, noted Christian apologist, was mad at God when his perfect girl was called away from him to God's service as a missionary. One year later, God brought him a more perfect (How about that for an oxymoron?) girl who became his wife. Ruth Graham said that had God answered her prayers, she would have married the wrong man... seven times! Countless tragedies have been prevented by God implementing drastic, distasteful measures in our life even though we were ticked off by His actions which seemed unfair or illogical. A missed promotion saved a marriage. An illness prevented us from self-destructing through unhealthy work habits. A relational struggle led to better management of conflict. A job layoff made us re-evaluate our priorities. A financial setback caused us to finally realize that we cannot serve both God and money.

Even when our lives are falling apart, God is working all things together for our good (Romans 8:28). He knows what the future holds, and what is best for us. Don't you think it's time we started trusting Him and stopped worrying about all the things over which we have no control? Do what God tells you to do. Take care of the things that He has placed in your control. Then rest in Him. Even when His work in our lives seems wrong, we can rest assured He is always right. His eye is on the sparrow, and I know He watches over you... and me.

"Heavenly Father, thank You for all the tragedies and heartaches I've missed because You were preventing them by Your grace and mercy. Forgive me for all my griping and complaining when things didn't turn out my way. You are God. I am not. I'm so glad. Your job is too hard. But You do it so well. Thanks for taking such good care of me. Amen."

17

Who among you fears the LORD and obeys His servant? If you are walking in darkness, without a ray of light, trust in the LORD and rely on your God. —Isaiah 50:10 NLT

One time after a long day of ministering to His sheep, Jesus said to His disciples, **"Let's get in the boat and go over to the other side of the lake."** And so they did. On the way, a fierce storm arose. The waves washed into the boat filling it to the point of sinking, but Jesus was sleeping in the back of the boat. In a panic, the disciples woke Him up. *"Lord, do you not care that we are all going to drown? Wake up and do something!"*

Jesus calmly arose, probably wiped the sleep from His eyes, and assessed the situation. Sternly and with great authority Jesus spoke to the waves, **"Quiet down!"** Immediately, the sea became like glass. Then Jesus turned His attention to His disciples. **"Why are you so afraid? Do you still not have faith in Me?"** (Mark 4:40 NLT).

Had I been there, I would have probably been in the same boat with the disciples. *"Yes, Lord, we have faith in You. It's this storm that's about to kill us that's causing us trouble."* I used to wonder why Jesus rebuked them for their lack of faith. Then one day, the Holy Spirit showed me something. Jesus told them before they ever got into the boat that they were going to the other side of the lake. How could they die in the middle of the sea if Jesus had already told them they were all going to the other side?

Fear, which is "**F**alse **E**vidence **A**ppearing **R**eal," rose up in the disciples' souls like the wind and waves of the storm. As the water filled the boat, fear filled their souls, and faith was washed overboard. It is easy to lose sight of the truth when the storms of life threaten to drown us. The truth of the matter is this... they were going to the other side. Jesus had said so. You can always count on His Word.

Beloved, are you walking in darkness right now? Are you having trouble hearing from the Lord? Has a storm of doubt risen up in your soul threatening to drown your faith? Don't doubt in the darkness what the Lord has shown you in the light. Has He not told you that you were going to the other side? Start bailing out your fear with these buckets of truth.

"I give them eternal life, and they will never perish. No one will snatch them away from Me, for My Father has given them to Me, and He is more powerful than anyone else. So no one can take them from Me" (John 10:28-30 NLT).

"I will never fail you. I will never forsake you." *That is why we can say with confidence, "The Lord is my helper, so I will not be afraid. What can mere mortals do to me?"* (Hebrews 13:5-6 NLT).

"Do not be afraid, for I have ransomed you. I have called you by name; you are Mine. When you go through deep waters and great trouble, I will be with you. When you go through rivers of difficulty, you will not drown! When you walk through the fire of oppression, you will not be burned up; the flames will not consume you. For I am the

LORD, your God, the Holy One of Israel, your Savior" (Isaiah 43:1-3 NLT).

"And I am convinced that nothing can ever separate us from His love. Death can't, and life can't. The angels can't, and the demons can't. Our fears for today, our worries about tomorrow, and even the powers of hell can't keep God's love away. Whether we are high above the sky or in the deepest ocean, nothing in all creation will ever be able to separate us from the love of God that is revealed in Christ Jesus our Lord" (Romans 8:38-39 NLT).

"Heavenly Father, what time I am afraid, I will trust in You no matter how dark it gets for darkness is light to You. Amen."

18

LORD, you are our Father. We are the clay, and You are the potter. We are all formed by Your hand. —Isaiah 64:8 NLT

There is a painting of a sculpture in which a man has been chiseled down to about his mid-thighs. His physique would make Arnold Schwartzeneggar green with envy. What makes the sculpture so interesting is that the sculpture and the sculptor are one and the same. The artist has placed the hammer and chisel in the hands of the statue. I guess he is the epitome of the "self-made man."

When I was a little boy... and I mean little... I used to dream of having a physique like Tarzan. You know, the washboard abs, the broad shoulders and bulging biceps. But alas, it was only a dream. I was in high school before I weighed 120 pounds. I remember always asking Mom and Dad what I could eat to make me gain weight. I would eat half a loaf of buttered toast at one sitting. I ate like there was no tomorrow, but I still never gained an ounce. As I child, my number one goal in life was to weigh over 100 pounds.

I was so desperate that I ordered a Charles Atlas bodybuilding course when I was about 12 years old. They sent me a few booklets and a bill for fifty dollars when fifty dollars was like five hundred. Scared me to death. I wrote the company a letter informing them that I was only twelve years old and didn't have fifty dollars. I never heard from them again, but the episode scared me so badly that it stunted my growth. I graduated from high school at my present height of six feet/one inch and a robust 148 pounds.

I couldn't understand for the life of me why God would not let me be like Tarzan. I prayed and begged Him, but He didn't seem to care if I looked like Cheetah rather than Tarzan. Then I began to grow. After thirty years, I reached the magical 200 pound mark. At forty, I reached 230 pounds. At fifty... that's enough of that. I guess my prayers were on time delay. I told Wanda the other day how blessed she was to have a bargain like me. I'm twice the man she married.

We are a fickle lot, aren't we? Today, I'm begging God to stop answering my childhood prayers. I'm like the guy who went out and sowed his wild oats and then prayed for crop failure. Adam and Eve thought it would be great to know good and evil like God, but that turned out to be a real bummer, too. There is something in us that makes us want to chisel our own statue, our own destiny, our own future. And God is so merciful and patient. He's willing to let us have our way if we persist. And He's so gentle and kind when we come crawling back to Him when things don't turn out the way we anticipated. He is a good God. Don't you just love Him?

I'm rapidly coming to the place in my life where I'm ready to drop my chisel and hammer and give myself back to the Master Sculptor. He saw the finished product before the foundation of the world. He knows just how much to chip off and how much to leave. He knows just where to sand me down and where to buff. He knows when I need a little abrasive tribulation and when I need the polish of encouragement. When He finishes with me, I know He will be pleased... and so will I. And if I don't get in His way, my statue will have a remarkable resemblance to Jesus. *"We can't even imagine what we will be like when Christ returns. But we do know*

that when He comes we will be like Him, for we will see Him as He really is." (1 John 3:2-3 NLT).
   Now, if I can only get out of His way.

"Heavenly Father, I'm an old 'chiseler' from way back. I've been sculpting me in my image rather than Yours. I am truly sorry. Will You take my chisel and hammer? I won't be needing them anymore. Thanks. Amen."

19

Let no one say when he is tempted, "I am tempted by God"; for God cannot be tempted by evil, nor does He Himself tempt anyone. But each one is tempted when he is drawn away by his own desires and enticed.
—James 1:13-14 NKJV

Clay and Kia, my beloved children, have always been close. They really love each other. However, they have had their moments. I remember one day when they were quietly playing in Clay's room. All of a sudden... BAM! The sound of shattered glass ricocheted through the house. I ran to see the damage. I threw open the door, and there they were sitting on the bed side by side like little angels. The lamp beside Clay's bed lay on the floor in little pieces.

"Okay. Who did it?" I began my inquisition. *"Not me!"* said Clay. *"Not me!"* Kia chimed in.

I looked around the room to see if I could find the real culprit. Some burglar must have snuck in the window and broke the lamp. Maybe the dog did it, but we didn't have a dog. I looked behind the door. I looked to see if the window was opened, and a tornado blew the lamp over. Alas, there was no one else in the room but Clay and Kia. I was puzzled because my kids always tell the truth. Don't yours?

I then addressed the suspects once more. *"Okay, you two are the only ones in the room. The lamp is broken, and I have serious doubts that it fell on the floor without some help. Now, I ask you again... who did it?"*

Once more I received the same reply. *"Not me!" "Not me!"*

"Alright, here's what I'm going to do. I'm going to count to three. If the one who broke the lamp does not confess, I'm going to spank you both. ONE... TWO..."

Kia panicked. "TELL HIM, CLAY! TELL HIM!"

Clay began to cry. He 'fessed up and received his just discipline. Kia dodged a bullet. I explained to both of them why Clay got a whipping. He was not punished because he broke the lamp. I'm sure it was an accident. But the fact that he lied about it was inexcusable.

Knowing the truth will set you free. Lies will keep you in bondage. *"**He that covers his sins will not prosper, but whoever confesses and forsakes them will have mercy**"* (Proverbs 28:13 NKJV). Whenever we experience difficulty and hard times, we are tempted to blame God. The serpent tempted Eve in the garden to blame God for withholding the good stuff. The flesh is our attempt to save our souls from humiliation. The flesh is prideful, deceitful and has no sense of need for anything, or anybody but self.

Notice how Adam and Eve responded when God caught them with their hand in the cookie jar... *God asked.* **"Have you eaten the fruit I commanded you not to eat?"**

"Yes," Adam admitted, "but it was the woman you gave me who brought me the fruit, and I ate it." Then the LORD God asked the woman,* "How could you do such a thing?" *"The serpent tricked me," she replied. "That's why I ate it." (Genesis 3:11-13 NLT).

The "blame game" is more popular than ever. *"It's my wife's fault. She never respects me." "If my husband would treat me better, I'd be a better wife." "I don't go to church anymore because the pastor didn't shake my hand the last time I was there." "I'm a good pastor. I just have a church full of stubborn sheep." "God, how could you do this to me?"*

God is love. It is impossible for Him to act toward us in any way other than perfect love. If hard times come, it is because God is trying to reveal to us areas of our lives that are unsurrendered to Him. The devil will tell you that if God really loved you, He wouldn't put you through this pain. Just the opposite is true, however. God uses the refining fire of hard times to remind us of our need to totally trust and depend upon Him. When the dross of self-sufficiency is burned away, we will begin to see that Jesus is all we need. Blaming God fogs up the window of our soul and frustrates our view of God.

Beloved, whenever your soul loses its peace and joy, stop and ask God what's wrong. He will tell you. When He does, crucify that lust of the flesh. ***"And those who are Christ's have crucified the flesh with its passions and desires. If we live in the Spirit, let us also walk in the Spirit"*** (Galatians 5:24-25 NKJV).

Whenever we point our finger of blame at God, or someone, or something else, there are three fingers pointing back at us. As long as we try to serve both our self interests and God, we will always live in doubt and confusion. We cannot serve two masters. The minute we surrender to Him and bring our agendas to the cross and completely rely upon Him, the cloud of confusion will lift, and we will see clearly the path He has laid before us. What joy and peace there is in trusting the Lord!

He is God. We are not. We must take responsibility for our attitudes and actions. God will take care of everyone else's. If this message sticks in your craw, don't blame me. Just bring your craw to the cross!

"Heavenly Father, I'm bringing my craw to You. Replace it with Your eternal perspective. Thanks for always knowing what I need and being patient with me until I realize it. Amen."

20

Thus says the LORD: "Cursed is the man who trusts in man and makes flesh his strength, whose heart departs from the LORD." —Jeremiah 17:5 NKJV

The "flesh" in this context is the residue of the "old man," or our "old sinful nature." Our "old man" was crucified with Christ. Romans 6:6-7 says, *"Knowing this, that our old man was crucified with Him, that the body of sin might be done away with, that we should no longer be slaves of sin. For he who has died has been freed from sin"* (NKJV). Our "old man" is dead. He died with Jesus on the cross. He is the one that was dead in trespasses and sins (Ephesians 2:1). He is the one who gets offended, becomes mad, pouts and acts contrary to the will and character of God.

Even though he is dead, we still remember how he lived. For instance... Suppose your father was verbally abusive and you could never do anything right in his eyes. Every time you made a mistake, he would scream at you and tell you how stupid you were. Then one day, your father dies. He cannot abuse you any longer. However, the next time you make a mistake, you run and hide for fear you'll be screamed at again. Your father is dead, but you react as if he is still alive. That is a residue from your father.

The flesh is the residue of your old man who died with Christ. Jesus set you free from the power of the old man. But if you respond to circumstances the same way you did before he died, you are living in the flesh. The Lord says that you are cursed when you let the flesh control your life. Heeding the desires of the flesh will destroy you. What is a saint to do? Glad you asked.

"And those who are Christ's have crucified the flesh with its passions and desires... If we live in the Spirit, let us also walk in the Spirit. I say then: Walk in the Spirit, and you shall not fulfill the lust of the flesh" (Gal 5:24-25; 16). Will your flesh ever cut you some slack? No. Will there ever come a time when choices are easy? No. We walk in the Spirit when we obey the Lord and His Word. If we do that, the flesh is denied its destructive influence. If you are waiting until you *feel* like walking in the Spirit, you are in for a long wait. The flesh will make sure of that.

Beloved, rain on your feelings. Step out on God's Word and act as if it's so, even if it's not so, so it can be so, because God said it is so. Feelings will line up with your faith once you step out and walk in it. How does that make you feel? See what I mean?

"Father, I get in trouble when I listen to my feelings. They lie sometimes. Help me to walk in Your Spirit today and put my flesh in its place... on the Cross. Thanks. Amen."

21

For see, today I have made you immune to their attacks.
—Jeremiah 1:18 NLT

I am a recovering people-pleaser. All my life I have looked to people to meet my needs. I told the Lord a long time ago that I wanted to spend my life helping hurting people. I believed that if I could fix other people then God might have mercy and fix me. It didn't work. God would not let me fix anybody because that's His business, not mine. Besides, anyone or anything we depend upon to meet our needs other than God is an idol. The Lord said that He would have no other gods before Him. Because He loved me so much, He frustrated every attempt I made to find purpose and meaning in life through the means of ministry. He knew what I really needed was Him... nothing more and nothing less. He is relentlessly faithful. Thank God that He is.

Since Wanda and I have been in the ministry, we have been abused, betrayed and rejected more times than Carter has liver pills. No matter how much we loved people and tried to meet their needs, ultimately they would get upset and abandon us. There were times when we begged God to take back His call upon our lives and let us live like normal people (You know that "normal" is just a setting on a clothes dryer.) Whenever we would start to throw a "pity party" and complain about how bad we had it, darkness and depression would engulf our spirits. There was no way out for us except to surrender totally to the Lord. But we did not surrender easily.

I finally came to realize that people could not fill the deep need of my heart, but I still kept hoping that someone would come through and love me as my soul longed to be loved. There were still some people we thought we could trust to hang in there with us no matter what. Then one day, those people told us that unless I changed they were leaving the church. I asked them how I needed to change. They simply said, *"You know what you need to change."* But I didn't know, and they wouldn't tell me. My last hope of finding a true friend who loved me all the time vanished like the morning fog. They left never relating exactly what I needed to change to "please" them. I was devastated.

At one of the lowest points in my life, the Lord woke me up at four o'clock in the morning. He directed me to get out of bed and look at Jeremiah chapter one. **"Get up and get dressed. Go out, and tell them whatever I tell you to say. Do not be afraid of them, or I will make you look foolish in front of them. For see, today I have made you immune to their attacks. You are strong like a fortified city that cannot be captured, like an iron pillar or a bronze wall. None of the kings, officials, priests, or people of Judah will be able to stand against you. They will try, but they will fail. For I am with you, and I will take care of you. I, the LORD, have spoken!"** (Jeremiah 1:17-19 NLT).

That wake-up call was a turning point in my life. God put me in a place where I had no where to go but to Him. I begged the Lord to forgive me for turning my back on Him and trusting in people. He graciously forgave me and put me in a graduate course on what it takes to be a soldier of the Cross. I discovered that night that the Cross is truly our Statue of Liberty. At the Cross, Jesus put on display His passion for Father God. I never understood why they called the last week of Christ's life, "Passion Week." The Lord Jesus' only passion was to please His Father. That was His secret. No amount of suffering, abuse, rejection and betrayal could dampen His zeal for Father's mission. Jesus was passionate about the Cross because it represented the ultimate act of obedience to the will and purpose of Father God.

The great men and women of God understood the secret of the life of immunity. The world sees the Cross as foolishness, but those who really love the Lord with a passion know it as the very power of God (I Corinthians 1:23-24). The Cross puts to death that old sinful man who came through the line of the first Adam. That old man is the source of all our trouble. It is he who hates to bow his knee to the Lordship of Jesus. When by faith we reckon him to be dead indeed, crucified with Christ, then and only then, does Christ begin to live powerfully in and through us. It is only through His Life that we can love as He loved, forgive our betrayers as He forgave, and obey God passionately as He obeyed.

The Cross is the place of immunity from all that would rob us of our identity and destiny. As we embrace the Cross, Christ lives full and free in us. Paul understood completely. *"For I determined not to know anything among you except Jesus Christ and Him crucified"* (1 Corinthians 2:1-2 NKJV). *"Yes, everything else is worthless when compared with the priceless gain of knowing Christ Jesus my Lord. I have discarded everything else, counting it all as garbage, so that I may have Christ"* (Philippians 3:8-9 NLT).

Some of us are so stubborn it takes a half century to realize that everything is worthless except Christ Jesus. Thank God for not giving up on us. Immunity from the world, the flesh and the devil lies at the foot of the Cross... the world's greatest garbage disposal. Dump ALL of yours there and begin to enjoy the priceless immunity that comes from being *"hid with Christ in God"* (Colossians 3:3).

"Lord, thank You that I am immune to the attacks of the devil through the Cross. As I embrace the Cross, I abide under the shadow of Your Almighty hand. It sure feels safe and comfortable here. Keep me here, Father. Amen."

22

"For I know the plans I have for you," says the LORD. "They are plans for good and not for disaster, to give you a future and a hope." —Jeremiah 29:11 NLT

God has a sovereign plan for your life and mine. He knows its beginning and its end as well as everything in between. He is God. We are not. How thankful we should be that He is a God of love, mercy, compassion, goodness, etc., etc., etc. He loves us and cares for us unconditionally even when we don't deserve it. He is a wonderful God.

His plan for each of us is tailor-made to provide the maximum glory for Him and the optimum fulfillment for us. *"You saw me before I was born. Every day of my life was recorded in Your book. Every moment was laid out before a single day had passed. How precious are Your thoughts about me, O God! They are innumerable! I can't even count them; they outnumber the grains of sand!"* (Psalm 139:16-18 NLT).

If God's plan is perfectly designed for our blessing and His glory, then why don't we follow it to the letter? Dr. Donald Grey Barnhouse gives an interesting analogy about that.

> *We will suppose the case of a man who loves violin music. He has the means to buy for himself a*

very fine violin, and he also purchases the very best radio obtainable. He builds up a library of the great musical scores, so that he is able to take any piece that is announced on the radio, put it on his music stand, and play along with the orchestra. The announcer says that Mr. Ormandy and the Philadelphia Orchestra are going to play Beethoven's seventh symphony. The man in his home puts that symphony on his stand and tunes his violin with what he hears coming from the orchestra. The music that comes from the radio we might call foreordained. Ormandy is going to follow the score just as Beethoven wrote it. The man in his living room starts to scratch away at the first violin part. He misses beats, he loses his place and finds it again, he breaks a string, and stops to fix it. The music goes on and on. He finds his place again and plays on after his fashion to the end of the symphony. The announcer names the next work that is to be played and the fiddler puts that number on his rack. Day after week after month after year, he finds pleasure in scraping his fiddle along with the violins of the great orchestras. Their music is determined in advance. What he must do is to learn to play in their tempo, in their key, and to follow the score as it has been written in advance. If he decides that he wants to play Yankee Doodle when the orchestra is in the midst of a Brahm's number, there's going to be dissonance and discord in the man's house but not in the Academy of Music. After some years of this, the man may be a rather creditable violin player and may have learned to submit himself utterly to the scores that are written and follow the program as played. Harmony and joy come from the submission and cooperation.

> *So it is with the plan of God. It is rolling toward us, unfolding day by day, as He has planned it before the foundation of the world. There are those who fight against it and who must ultimately be cast into outer darkness because He will not have in His heaven those who proudly resist Him. This cannot be tolerated any more than the authorities would permit a man to bring his own violin into the Academy of Music and start to play Shostakovich when the program called for Bach. The score of God's plan is set forth in the Bible. In the measure that I learn it, submit myself to it, and seek to live in accordance with all that is therein set forth, I shall find myself in joy and in harmony with God and His plans. If I set myself to fight against it, or disagree with that which comes forth, there can be no peace in my heart and life. If in my heart I seek to play a tune that is not the melody the Lord has for me, there can be nothing but dissonance. Prayer is learning to play the tune that the eternal plan of God calls for and to do that which is in harmony with the will of the Eternal Composer and the Author of all that is true harmony in life and living.* (Man's Ruin: Romans 1:1-32 [Grand Rapids: Eerdmans, 1952], pp. 122-23. Used by permission.)

You can play, *I Did It My Way*, while God is playing His song if you like, but it will sound terrible, make you miserable and hurt everybody's ears. Father God wants you to make music with Him... not for Him. He's already written the words and music. Stop fiddling around and play... magnificently!

"Heavenly Father, You are the great Composer. What a melody you have written for me. How sweet and harmonic. Tune me up so that the world will be able to 'name that tune' and join in the symphony. Bravo! Encore! Amen!"

23

But You, O God, do see trouble and grief; You consider it to take it in hand. The victim commits himself to You; You are the helper of the fatherless. —Psalm 10:14 NIV

I am extremely allergic to cats. I can walk into a room where a cat lives and within five minutes my eyes swell shut and my nose runs like a greyhound. I don't have anything against cats, but we don't get along very well from a physiological point of view. This past week we helped Kia move into her apartment in Greensboro. I had forgotten that she had rescued a homeless cat she had found wandering around the neighborhood. She named him Moses. Appropriate, don't you think? When I opened the door, there sat Moses in all his splendor. Immediately my eyes began to itch, my nose stopped up, and I knew I was in trouble. For two days I swelled shut and walked around like a zombie doped up on Benedryl.

We left on Thursday. By Saturday, I could breathe again, and you could start to see the whites of my eyes. That afternoon we attended a baby shower. On the way, I spied a fur ball on the edge of the road. At first glance, I thought it was a big rat or a white squirrel. As we drew alongside the animal, I ascertained that it was a kitten. Then I made my big mistake. *"That's a kitten."* Wanda didn't see it. If only I had kept my mouth shut. *"Oh! Go back and get it! Honey, it will die out there in the road!"*

When the Word says that husbands are to love their wives like Christ loved the Church, I didn't think He meant picking up allergy bombs on the roadside. Anyway, we picked up the kitten and took her to the shower. She looked like she had just emerged from a shower... soaking wet, eyes swelled shut, shivering like a ten penny finishing nail hit by a greasy ballpein hammer. At first we thought she had been hit by a car. We finally decided that she had just been thrown away because one eye looked really bad. Nobody wants a cat with a defect. I can't understand why anyone would want a cat anyway... especially me.

Needless to say, we have a new baby at our house. My eyes look like a road map again, and Wanda walks around the house holding her "grand-cat" and talking baby-talk. MiMi (Wanda's grandma name) is craving grandchildren, but I hope when we have some they won't swell my head up like a balloon unless it's pride.

We named her Yoda, because she looks like the little creature in the Star Wars movie. I know the force is with her because it's strong enough to knock me down. After three days of intensive care, two prescriptions and a $57 vet bill, Yoda is looking better. Her eye is opening up a little, and she eats like a horse. Snuggles mothers her and Wanda nurses her. I just sit in the den, blow my nose, scratch my eyes and keep my mouth shut.

It's amazing how much better you can hear the Lord when you keep your mouth shut. God has used Yoda to remind me of how much He loves me and how much He suffered on my behalf. He found me one day stranded, abandoned, blinded, cold, shivering and lost. He took me in even though He was allergic to my sin. He was willing to endure the pain and affliction my sin caused Him because He had compassion on me. Compassion is simply love mingled with sorrow. I was

Jesus... My Final Answer

as helpless and as hopeless as Yoda was the day we found her. He didn't have to come down here and save me, but He did. *"He was wounded and crushed for our sins. He was beaten that we might have peace. He was whipped, and we were healed! All of us have strayed away like sheep. We have left God's paths to follow our own. Yet the LORD laid on Him the guilt and sins of us all. He was oppressed and treated harshly, yet He never said a word. He was led as a lamb to the slaughter. And as a sheep is silent before the shearers, He did not open His mouth"* (Isaiah 53:4-7 NLT).

Our Father sees all our trouble and grief and is not afraid to get His hands dirty with us. The hands that bore the nails are not afraid of a little crud from a sin-sick world. He takes us in hand and cares for us, paying our sin debt and healing us by His stripes. He went way out of His way to bring us hope when we were hopeless... help when we were helpless... sight when we were blind... healing when we were dying. If a human heart can show love and compassion for a worthless fur ball like Yoda, think how much the perfect heart of the perfect God can love us back to life. If you don't know His love, He's waiting patiently to give it. If you know His love, rest in His embrace and enjoy it. Yoda knows what a little love can do.... puuurrrrfectly well!

"Lord, thank You for stopping to pick me up when I was lost and dying. You didn't have to do it, but You saw my distress and came to my rescue even though in doing so, I caused You much pain and heartache. May the life You gave me and the life I live today be worthy of the price You paid for me. I love You, Lord. Amen."

24

Yes, ask anything in My Name, and I will do it!
—*John* 14:14 NLT

Father has blessed me with over thirty-three wonderful years with my precious Bride. We have enjoyed some absolutely blissful moments, and we have weathered some pretty intense storms from within and without. By the grace of God, all of our experiences have polished us rather than grinding us down. He is a good God.

During this time, I have come to know my wife pretty well. I've seen her at her best and at her worst which is better than most people's best. She is a gem. I know what she likes and doesn't like. I know what turns her on and what turns her off. I know she doesn't like her feet tickled, livermush, or people who don't pull their own weight. She loves for me to read the Bible to her and play with her hair until she falls asleep. She is a night owl and doesn't do mornings except when we are getting up early to go to the beach. Banana splits with nuts and three cherries, decorating her house, and entertaining people at home are some of her favorite things. Cooking is not her passion although she is an excellent cook when necessary. Having survived years of living first with a teacher/coach and now with a preacher, she has a wealth of wisdom and experience for young women embarking upon their maiden voyage into marital bliss. She is an excellent mother. She prays constantly for her children and would buy them the world if she had the money. If she has a fault, she probably worries about her kids too much.

There are tons of other things I could say about my Bride, but that would take another book or two. My point is this: I know her. I know how she thinks. I know what makes her happy and what makes her sad. I know what she doesn't want, what she does want, and when she wants it. I can speak on her behalf because I know how she would respond if she were able to do so herself. That is what Jesus meant when He told us to ask in His Name.

The key to prayer is knowing what the Lord wants, when He wants it, and what He doesn't want. Prayer is the means whereby we get to know our Lord. I got to know Wanda very well by being with her, talking with her, fussing and discussing with her, studying her. I ask a lot of questions. Her answers tell me much about herself. If we are to glorify the Lord through our prayers, then we must know Him intimately. We must have His mind, His thoughts, His desires, His heart. Then we can ask in His Name... as if He were asking Himself... and He will answer so that the Father might be glorified in the Son.

The Apostle Paul's heartcry was to know the Lord. ***"I want to know Christ and the power of His resurrection and the fellowship of sharing in His sufferings"*** (Philippians 3:10 NIV). Paul understood that we get to know one another by hanging in there together in both good times and bad. That's how we get to know Him. We laugh with Him, cry with Him, inquire of Him, joke with Him and hang out with Him. Then we can pray as He would pray. And you know when Jesus prays, Father God listens. If we want His ear, then we must pray as Jesus would. Jesus only asked for what His Father wanted Him to ask for. In order to do that, we must know Him as Jesus knew His Father.

"Heavenly Father, I realize that most of my prayers focus on what I want rather than what You want. I try to make it sound like it's what You want by tacking "in Jesus' Name" on the end of my prayer. Please forgive me for asking for things You don't want and for not asking for things You do. Lord, can we hang out together so I can get to know You better? Maybe then, I can become a better pray-er when I know You better. Thanks for Your patience and understanding. Lord, teach me to pray. I think I can ask that in Your Name, can I not? Amen."

25

He cuts off every branch that doesn't produce fruit, and He prunes the branches that do bear fruit so they will produce even more. —John 15:2 NLT

We have two oak trees in our backyard about 30 to 35 feet tall. I have my hammock between them. It is under those trees that the Lord has given me much direction and insight. I ought to spend more time out there in my hammock, but that's not my point. As I recline in that hammock and gaze up through the trees, I notice that there are hundreds of small branches that sprout in all directions from the major branches. In mid-summer there are no leaves or signs of life in those twigs. The life-giving sun cannot penetrate the thick cover of leaves enshrouding the tree. Without sunlight those tiny branches are doomed from the git-go. Over the years there have been a multitude of sprouts which had fired and fallen back. I'm sure each one believed that they would grow and develop into a huge branch just like the one from which they had sprouted. The interior of those trees looks like a graveyard of skinny, dead, unsightly branches gnarled and twisted as they sought in vain to survive.

The Lord had spoken to me on many occasions that I needed to prune those branches to improve the health of the tree. Not only did I need to prune away the dead branches,

I also needed to prune back the good healthy ones that were blocking the sunlight from reaching the interior of the tree. Whenever the Lord would speak to me about the matter, I would agree with Him that I needed to do that, but alas, I never found the time.

Then one December, we had the worst ice storm in decades. Because the trees still had most of their leaves, the ice was brutal. Limbs and major branches couldn't sustain the weight of all that frozen moisture and succumbed to the pressure. All those dead and weak branches and even some of the good ones who were weak due to a lack of pruning snapped and broke. Over a million people in North Carolina were out of electricity for days. Trees have no respect for power lines, houses, cars or anything else that happens to be under them when they fall. Power companies are well aware of the consequences of allowing tree branches to hover over power lines. They are constantly pruning trees in the heat of the summer in anticipation of ice storms in the winter. An ounce of prevention is worth a pound of cure. Believe me, I know that after a full day of chain sawing and hauling limbs.

The Lord used this ice storm and all my fallen branches to remind me that I need pruning as well. We all do. I don't know about you, but my life is strewn with dead branches of activities and projects that started out with high hopes but died due to lack of Sonlight and direction from the Lord. They sounded so good at the time, but they were basically my ideas, not His. I've learned that God does not *appreciate* what He does not *initiate*. But He never says, *"I told you so,"* nor does He ever rub my nose in my mistakes. He simply says, **"Kenny, there's a lot of clutter in your life that's zapping all your strength and energy. There are some really good things you are doing that need thinning out as well. Let's get rid of some of this dead weight. What do you say?"**

If I don't take the initiative myself to do the pruning, then He will allow ice storms of trial and tribulation to encourage me to do so. When the ice came, I had to make pruning a priority. I couldn't drive my car with a tree on top of it. It's amazing how a good storm will rearrange your priorities.

We may have another ice storm or two this winter, but I'm not worried. The branches that are left are strong enough now to survive without breaking. Isn't it funny how we murmur and complain about the hard times we are called to endure when God's reason for sending them is to simply prune off the superfluous stuff in our lives that magnifies our misery during the storms of life. Ice storms and trials are God's little love gifts to us. He knows that pruning may be painful at the moment, but the pain will bring the gain of strength, peace and confidence when the next storm strikes. And like the weather, life is a succession of blue skies and storms. Pruning keeps us healthy and strong for both.

"Father God, thanks for pruning me. Don't stop even when I yell and scream. I know that I have a lot of dead branches in me that are zapping my strength and stifling Your life within me. Show me the branches You want removed. You are free to cut off any branch... even the ones that I might deem irreplaceable. You are my tree trunk. I'm simply a branch. I have no life apart from You. Give me the grace to stay firmly rooted in You. Thanks. Amen."

26

Listen, my child, to what your father teaches you. Don't neglect your mother's teaching. What you learn from them will crown you with grace and clothe you with honor.
—Proverbs 1:8-9 NLT

∼

Do you know the first requirement for salvation from your sins? Admitting that you are a sinner and taking responsibility for the choices you make. The Lord is little by little revealing to me the ploy of the devil. Our adversary is incessantly whispering into people's ears, *"It's not your fault. You don't have to accept responsibility for the choices you make and the way you live. You are your own god. To heck with everyone else. Do your own thing."*

That lie goes back to the Garden of Eden. Remember how Adam and Eve responded after they bought the devil's lie and ate the forbidden fruit? ***The LORD God asked, "Have you eaten the fruit I commanded you not to eat?"***

"Yes," Adam admitted, "but it was the woman you gave me who brought me the fruit, and I ate it."

Then the LORD God asked the woman, "How could you do such a thing?"

"The serpent tricked me," she replied. "That's why I ate it." (Genesis 3:11-13 NLT).

Notice that Adam blamed Eve, but in reality, he was blaming God. *"It was the woman YOU gave me. If You had not given me that woman, I would have never eaten the fruit."* Yeah, right. Eve blamed the serpent, and the serpent didn't have a leg to stand on. The "blame game" has been played for eons and is still very popular today. I watched a television program the other night in which a parent sued a beer company because their advertisements lured their teenage son into alcoholism and killed him.

I'm not an advocate for the alcohol industry. I've seen too much misery from the stuff. But excuse me... did they make that boy drink beer? What if their advertisements made it look like drinking beer would meet his emotional needs for acceptance, was it not still his choice to drink it? Television makes illicit sex and adultery appear to be okay, but does that give me an excuse for being unfaithful to my wife? What is the world coming to? Where have we gone wrong? I'm a little homesick for some old-fashioned values that are learned in the school of hard knocks. I like what Paul Harvey has to say...

We tried so hard to make things better for our kids that we made them worse. For my grandchildren, I'd like better.

I'd really like for them to know about hand me down clothes and homemade ice cream and leftover meat loaf sandwiches. I really would.

I hope you learn humility by being humiliated, and that you learn honesty by being cheated.

I hope you learn to make your own bed and mow the lawn and wash the car.

And I really hope nobody gives you a brand new car when you are sixteen.

It will be good if at least one time you can see puppies born and your old dog put to sleep.

I hope you get a black eye fighting for something you believe in.

I hope you have to share a bedroom with your younger brother/sister. And it's all right if you have to draw a line

Jesus... My Final Answer

down the middle of the room, but when he wants to crawl under the covers with you because he's scared, I hope you let him.

When you want to see a movie and your little brother/sister wants to tag along, I hope you'll let him/her. I hope you have to walk uphill to school with your friends and that you live in a town where you can do it safely.

On rainy days when you have to catch a ride, I hope you don't ask your driver to drop you two blocks away so you won't be seen riding with someone as uncool as your Mom.

If you want a slingshot, I hope your Dad teaches you how to make one instead of buying one.

I hope you learn to dig in the dirt and read books.

When you learn to use computers, I hope you also learn to add and subtract in your head.

I hope you get teased by your friends when you have your first crush on a boy/girl, and when you talk back to your mother that you learn what ivory soap tastes like.

May you skin your knee climbing a mountain, burn your hand on a stove and stick your tongue on a frozen flagpole.

I don't care if you try a beer once, but I hope you don't like it. And if a friend offers you dope or a joint, I hope you realize he is not your friend.

I sure hope you make time to sit on a porch with your Grandma/Grandpa and go fishing with your Uncle.

May you feel sorrow at a funeral and joy during the holidays.

I hope your mother punishes you when you throw a baseball through your neighbor's window and that she hugs you and kisses you at Hanukkah/Christmas time when you give her a plaster mold of your hand.

These things I wish for you — tough times and disappointment, hard work and happiness. To me, it's the only way to appreciate life.

One reason the Lord Jesus died on the cross was to give us a choice. Before Christ came and paid our sin debt on the cross, we had no choice. We were blind and bound by sin, taken captive by the devil to do his will. When Jesus came with His gift of salvation, He merely opened the door to our cage. Whether we fly out to freedom, or remain imprisoned is our choice. God has made a way. We are responsible to accept or reject His offer. And we must live eternally with the consequences of the choice we make. The tough times, disappointments and heartaches of life make the choice easy for me. What about you?

"Heavenly Father, what a wonderful God You are. I thank You for allowing me to experience the pain of my poor choices. That pain has made Your grace and love so marvelously apparent and appealing to me. Thanks for opening the door to my cage. Thanks for the wings to fly out. Thanks for the winds of adversity that lift me above my circumstances and closer to You. Amen."

27

Jesus replied, "If I want him to remain alive until I return, what is that to you? You follow Me." —John 21:22-23 NLT

Jesus had just finished His reconciliation supper with Peter. At the Last Supper, Jesus told His disciples that one of them would betray Him. They were all astonished, especially Peter... *"If all these forsake You, I won't! I'll die for You!"* Jesus calmly told Peter that before the rooster crowed in the morning, he would have denied His Lord three times.

As they reclined around the fire after this supper, the Lord asked Peter... **"Simon, son of John, do you love me more than these** (referring to the other disciples)?" Whenever Peter acted like his old nature, Jesus would always refer to him as Simon. Jesus asked Peter three times if he loved Him. Peter was grieved because he was afraid to shoot off his mouth again.

Then Jesus revealed to Peter that he was, indeed, going to die for Him. Then the Lord simply said, **"Follow me."** Doesn't sound much like the gospel we hear preached today, does it? Today's false gospel makes Jesus a nice addition to your repertoire. I've heard people preach that Jesus is your buddy, your great Santa Claus in the sky. Pull Him out of your pocket whenever you need Him. He will meet all your needs, which being interpreted means all your wants. You can still live and let Jesus have whatever is left. He appreciates anything and any time you have to spare.

Beloved, Jesus died for you and for me. He left all the glory and bliss of heaven to come here in the muck and mire of sin, rebellion and selfishness to be beaten, spit upon and crucified to keep us from spending eternity in hell. How dare we let Him bear the cross alone so that we can live footloose and fancy free to indulge in our own pleasure. Jesus is our Life. Without Him, we are dead in our own trespasses and sin, hopeless and undone. How desperately we need to be brought to the awareness of our absolute need for Christ.

Salvation is not just an invitation to go to heaven when we die even though that comes with it. Salvation is an invitation to come and die to everything that is not in God's plan for us. And He has a specific plan and destiny for each and every one of us. When we receive Him as our Life, we give up the rights to our own. He, and He alone, has the right to determine the course and direction for our lives. But we don't like that, do we? Peter didn't like it either.

"Okay, Lord, so I'm going to die for You, but what are You going to do with John?" Peter inquired.

Jesus replied, **"If I want John to stay here until I return again, what is that to you. You follow Me."**

It doesn't matter what He does with anyone else. That's between them and the Lord. The destiny the Lord has placed in me has a time, route and destination prepared just for me and me alone. He has a unique plan for you, too. We have no right to dictate to Him what we will, or will not allow. He alone has that right. We gave our rights up the day we chose to follow Him.

"Lord, I am so weak. One minute, I say I will follow You no matter where You lead. The next minute, I'm griping because I don't like the bumpy road You chose. I don't know what's best for me. I really don't care. I do care that my life is not

spent in vain. I want all that I do to glorify You no matter what. You lead. I will follow. If I get off track, jerk me back onto the narrow road less-traveled. I don't know how You plan to get me there, but I do know where I'm going. For that, I am eternally grateful. Amen."

28

Jesus replied, "I assure you, unless you are born again, you can never see the Kingdom of God." —John 3:3 NLT

I am a human being by birth. Rabbits are rabbits by birth. Gorillas are gorillas by birth. I don't act like a human being in order to become one. Rabbits don't hop around so that they can become a rabbit. And I will never be a gorilla by walking around dragging my knuckles on the ground and beating my chest even though Wanda says I act that way sometimes. All God's living creatures are who they are by birth, not by actions.

Then why do we think that acting like a Christian will make us one? We are Christians, children of God by birth, not by our actions and behavior. Yes, humans do act like animals sometimes and gorillas act like humans, but that does not change their natures. Jesus said, **"You must be born again."** We are who we are by birth... period!

Now I'm not saying that our actions and behavior are not important. I'm just saying that we act and behave the way we do because of the nature of our birth. I can hop around like a rabbit for awhile, but I'll be miserable because I'm not made to hop. It goes against my grain. As a born again child of God, I can act contrary to my nature for a while (sin), but I'll be miserable. Pigs love mudholes. Sheep do not. Sheep may fall into a mudhole occasionally, but they hate it after a while because sheep don't like to get muddy.

Beloved, you don't have to try to act like a child of God. You ARE a blood-bought child of God purchased with the precious blood of the Lamb, our Lord and Savior, Christ Jesus. He made us. You don't have to act anymore. God birthed you by "supernatural childbirth." Now, just BE who you are... naturally.

"Father, thank You that all I have to do to please you is to BE who You created me to be. Whenever I try to be something different, there is a gap in the world. No one can be who You created me to be. No one can take my place. Thanks for making me unique and uniquely gifted to serve You like no other. Amen."

29

Jesus has become our eternal High Priest in the line of Melchizedek. —Hebrews 6:20 NLT

Embedded in the seventh chapter of the book of Hebrews is the key to understanding the awesomeness of the Gospel and what Jesus accomplished for us. Let's take a look. *"This Melchizedek was king of the city of Salem and also a priest of God Most High. When Abraham was returning home after winning a great battle against many kings, Melchizedek met him and blessed him. Then Abraham took a tenth of all he had won in the battle and gave it to Melchizedek. His name means "king of justice." He is also "king of peace" because Salem means "peace." There is no record of his father or mother or any of his ancestors--no beginning or end to his life. He remains a priest forever, resembling the Son of God"* (Hebrews 7:1-3 NLT).

Melchizedek was a type of Christ. He was not Christ, but he did foreshadow what Jesus would be like when He came. You can read the entire account of Abraham's encounter with Melchizedek in Hebrews chapter 7. For the sake of time and space, allow me to give you the KAV (Kenny's Authorized Version).

Abraham goes out and whips up on these kings who came against him. After the battle, this High Priest of the

Most High God comes out of nowhere. It's the first and only time he shows up according to the Bible. In honor of the Lord, Abraham pays Melchizedek a tithe (a tenth) of all the spoils he had taken from the kings he had defeated. The Scripture goes on the say that Levi, Abraham's great-grandson, also paid tithes to Melchizedek (Hebrews 7:9-10). Now how could Levi pay tithes to Melchizedek if this is the High Priest's only appearance, and Levi is not even born yet? The Word says that Levi received credit for paying tithes to Melchizedek because when Abraham paid them, Levi was in the loins of Abraham. Wow! Do you see the implications of that? If not, allow me to explain the "Good News."

Ephesians 1:4 says, *"Long ago, even before He made the world, God loved us and chose us in Christ to be holy and without fault in His eyes"* (NLT). Father God knew you before He even created the world. He knew you were a mess, and He chose you anyway. He loved you so much that He placed you in the "loins" of His Son, Jesus Christ. That simply means that whatever Jesus did, you got credit for it. Is that not amazing?

Jesus said in the Sermon on the Mount, *"But you are to be perfect, even as your Father in heaven is perfect"* (Matthew 5:48 NLT). How in the world can we be perfect? We were flawed when we got here. That verse messed with my mind for years until God revealed the Gospel through Melchizedek. Jesus lived a perfect life. He never sinned a single time. Since we were in His loins when He lived that perfect life, we got credit for it just as if we had done it ourselves. We didn't and couldn't do it, but God treats us as if we did because Christ did it for us. Understand?

It gets better. Romans 6:23 says, *"For the wages of sin is death, but the free gift of God is eternal life through Christ Jesus our Lord"* (NLT). If we have to pay for our sin, the price is death... eternal separation from God. Since God is Life, if we are separated from Him, then we are dead.

Jesus paid the wages of our sin when He died on the Cross. Everyone who sins must pay with His life. Since we were in Christ when He died, we got credit for paying those wages as if we had died. Jesus died in our place, paid the bill and gave us His Life. *"Once you were dead, doomed forever because of your many sins. But God is so rich in mercy, and He loved us so very much, that even while we were dead because of our sins, He gave us life when He raised Christ from the dead"* (Ephesians 2:1&5 NLT). Wow!

Now this will blow your mind! *"For He raised us from the dead along with Christ, and we are seated with Him in the heavenly realms--all because we are one with Christ Jesus"* (Ephesians 2:6 NLT). If Jesus is seated in Heaven along with Father God, and we are in Christ, then where are we? We are in heaven with Jesus right now! When we finally get to heaven and see Him face-to-face, it will boggle our minds to know that we have been there in Heaven with Him all along! How good is that?

If Jesus is in Heaven and everything is under His feet, then everything is under our feet as well. That means that we should never be on bottom... the bottom of our circumstances... the bottom of our problems. And especially on the bottom of satan's feet. We are overcomers because Jesus overcame and triumphed over sin, the world and the devil. We are free, indeed! We are more than conquerors in Him!

Please note that we did not do or accomplish any of this. Jesus did it all. When we by faith believe (cling to, trust in, rely upon, put our whole weight upon) in Christ Jesus as Lord and Savior, all that He is and did becomes ours as well. Blessed be our Lord Jesus! Hail to the King! He alone is worthy of our honor and praise!

The question now is this: Have you put your whole trust in the Lord? Or are you still trying to earn your own salvation through your own efforts? Jesus paid it all. All to Him we owe. We were bought at a great price... the blood of Jesus.

We are no longer our own. He has every right to us. Don't you think it's time you pay up and give Him what He paid for? Are you ready?

"Heavenly Father, how could I ever thank You for loving me so much that You chose me before the world began and placed me in Your Son, Jesus? Lord Jesus, thank You for living a perfect life for me. Thank You for dying in my place. Thank You for forgiving my sins and washing them away with Your precious blood. Right now, I ask You to take Your rightful place on the throne of my heart. I confess You as Lord of my life and without a doubt believe that You rose from the dead. May my life glorify You from this day forth in all that I do and say. Thank You for giving me Your Life when I was dead in trespasses and sin. Thank You for saving me from being separated from You forever. I love you! Amen!"

30

Today I have given you the choice between life and death, between blessings and curses. I call on heaven and earth to witness the choice you make. Oh, that you would choose life, that you and your descendants might live!
—Deuteronomy 30:19-20 NLT

She is ninety-two years old, petite, well poised and proud. She is fully dressed each morning by eight o'clock with her hair fashionably coifed, and her makeup perfectly applied in spite of the fact she is legally blind. Today she has moved to a nursing home. Her husband of 70 years recently passed away making this move necessary. After many hours of waiting patiently in the lobby of the nursing home where I am employed, she smiled sweetly when told her room was ready. As she maneuvered her walker to the elevator, I provided a visual description of her tiny room, including the eyelet curtains that had been hung on her window. *"I love it,"* she stated with the enthusiasm of an eight-year-old having just been presented with a new puppy. *"Mrs. Jones, you haven't seen the room... just wait,"* I said.

Then she spoke these words that I will never forget:

"That does not have anything to do with it," she gently replied. *"Happiness is something you decide*

on ahead of time. Whether I like my room or not, does not depend on how the furniture is arranged. It is how I arrange my mind. I have already decided to love it. It is a decision I make every morning when I wake up. I have a choice. I can spend the day in bed recounting the difficulty I have with the parts of my body that no longer work, or I can get out of bed and be thankful for the ones that do work. Each day is a gift, and as long as my eyes open, I will focus on the new day and all of the happy memories I have stored away just for this time in my life. Old age is like a bank account. You withdraw from what you have already put in. I believe that our background and circumstances may have influenced who we are, but we are responsible for who we become. I believe that no matter how good a friend is, they're going to hurt you every once in a while, and you must forgive them for that. I believe that just because someone doesn't love you the way you want them to doesn't mean they don't love you with all they have. I believe that true friendship continues to grow even over the longest distance. Same goes for true love. I believe that it's taking me a long time to become the person I want to be. I believe that you should always leave loved ones with loving words. It may be the last time you see them. I believe that you can keep going long after you can't. I believe that the people you care about most in life are taken from you too soon. I believe that we should never take God's blessings for granted... especially those He has put into our lives to love us and to be loved by us. I believe our quality of life is determined by the choices we make. Life is a choice. We must choose wisely." (source unknown).

Jesus... My Final Answer

I have said before that the people who have influenced my life the most are not the people I believe in, but the people who believe in me. I heard an interview last night on *Focus on the Family*. A young man was on the program who had been abused in every way possible as a child while staying in a foster home. He related how a man, an ordinary man, took an interest in him. This man, whom he called "Grandpa" although not a blood relative, believed in him. Grandpa encouraged him to reach for the stars... to dream the impossible dream. Grandpa believed in the boy and encouraged him. By the way, encouragement means to put courage into people so that they will overcome their doubts and fears and step out into their destinies.

Today that young man has graduated from college, divinity school and a school of the arts. He is writing scripts for Christian movies today that I'm sure God will use to touch untold numbers of lives all because one solitary Grandpa believed in the destiny of one downtrodden little boy. I believe God put us here to make a difference in the world... one downtrodden life at a time.

I believe in you. I believe you are special because God made you special. You have a divine purpose. Maybe your purpose is just to spread a little sunshine in a dark world, or maybe you could be the next Billy Graham. No matter. Sunshine spreaders and world-class evangelists are no different in God's sight. Both are just as precious to Him. Now go out there today and brighten up this place. We are the light of the world, you know. Jesus said so. Shine, Beloved, shine!

"Heavenly Father, help me today to choose wisely the course of my life. Help me to light at least one little candle and keep me from cursing the darkness. You are the Light of my life. I don't want to put a basket over You. I want You to set me in places today so that Your Light will shine for all to see. You choose the places. I'll do the shining. Amen."

31

Then Jesus asked the man, "What do you want Me to do for you?" —Luke 18:41 NLT

This question was addressed to a blind beggar on the side of the road who shouted for the Lord to have mercy on him as Jesus passed by on the way to Jericho. People standing around the blind beggar told him to shut up, but he shouted even louder. When Jesus heard him, He stopped and popped the question... **"What do you want Me to do for you?"** *"Lord, I want to see!"* the beggar pleaded.

The beggar was sick and tired of the misery of blindness. He was desperate. I guess so. Can you imagine having to sit on the side of the road never being able to see what's going on around you and having to depend upon the mercy of other people to survive? You know how people are. You and I are one of them. We are selfish, self-absorbed and generally merciless. But Jesus is the antithesis of us. He is totally selfless, Father God-absorbed and His mercy endures forever. The Lord showed mercy to this blind beggar by allowing him to come to the point of utter hopelessness until he had only one Hope. Until we have exhausted every other avenue of survival, we will never find the Blessed Hope. The pride of self-sufficiency blinds us to the realization that Jesus is not only the Final Answer... He is the ONLY Answer.

When God in His mercy brought the beggar to the point of desperation, he cried out with an intensity that caught the Lord's attention. The tone of a baby's cry determines the response of the mother. A wimper barely turns her head, but a piercing cry brings mama running. I believe the Lord watches to see how serious... how desperate we are for Him, not just for what He can do for us. The Psalmist said, *"I cried out to the LORD in my suffering, and He heard me. He set me free from all my fears"* (Psalm 34:6 NLT).

Beloved, what is blinding you from seeing Jesus? Sin? Pride? Ambition? Bitterness? Unforgiveness? A painful past? Reputation? Rebellion? Are you facing a seemingly impossible situation and have resigned yourself to the fact that it is hopeless? Listen... there is no such thing as a hopeless situation... only faithless people who have grown hopeless about it. Are you willing to let Jesus open your blinded eyes and see what He sees? What you see about yourself will make you desperate to be free from the sickening meaningless of life apart from Him. The question is... Will it make you sick enough to surrender unconditionally to Him?

What is it you want Jesus to do for *you*?

"Dear Lord, I want to be free from me. As Pogo once said, "We have met the enemy and he is US!" I am my own worst enemy. I... I... I.... It's all about me, not You. I want to be free from the prison of self. I have a lot of questions, but I want you to be my Final Answer and that will be enough for me. Amen."

32

Then they willingly received Him into the boat, and immediately the boat was at the land where they were going.
—John 6:21 NKJV

Jesus had just fed five thousand men, not counting the women and children, with five barley loaves and two small fish. His miracle caused quite a stir. People began to jump on the band wagon. *"This is the Prophet we've been looking for!"* Jesus, knowing that many of those who dined that day were more interested in fish and chips than surrendering their hearts to Him as Lord and Messiah, departed to the mountain to be alone. Meanwhile, His disciples could wait no longer to get back to headquarters. They jumped into their boat and headed out across the Sea of Galilee toward Capernaum. Let's recount the story.

"Now when evening came, His disciples went down to the sea, got into the boat, and went over the sea toward Capernaum. And it was already dark, and Jesus had not come to them. Then the sea arose because a great wind was blowing. So when they had rowed about three or four miles, they saw Jesus walking on the sea and drawing near the boat; and they were afraid. But He said to them, 'It is I; do not be afraid.' Then they willingly received Him into

the boat, and immediately the boat was at the land where they were going" (John 6:16-21 NKJV).

Have you ever been in such a hurry you just couldn't wait on the Lord? You prayed, begged, bargained and maybe even fasted, and the Lord just didn't give you the answer you were looking for? So you ran ahead and acted without a word from the Lord. Your way became dark. Winds of confusion and doubt began to blow with gale force. And then when the Answer came walking toward you on the angry waters of your self-made dilemma, you were scared to death and didn't even recognize Him. Know what I mean?

Don't feel like the Lone Ranger. His disciples, who got to know Him up close and personal, still became antsy and ran ahead without Him. Whenever we leave Jesus behind, fear assaults us. Jesus is the Truth. Fear is **f**alse **e**vidence **a**ppearing **r**eal. It causes us to believe lies and to think very pessimistically. Someone has said that fear is the darkroom where the devil develops our negatives.

It was getting dark, and they thought they couldn't make it across without light. Their fear blinded them to the fact that Jesus was the Light of the World. If they had Him with them, they would have never been in darkness. But how precious is Jesus! He comes out to them in the midst of their mess. It was all their own fault for not waiting on Him, and yet He has compassion on them. **"Don't be afraid. It's just Me."**

In all my years of counseling, I've told people the Truth until I'm blue in the face. Most of the time it just bounces off of them like a BB off a rhinoceros. Then one day, Jesus comes and speaks His Truth and the penny drops. Head knowledge becomes heart knowledge. Darkness is expelled as the Light of His Truth floods their soul. It's the same Truth I've told them a million times, but when He speaks it... Oh, the difference!

When Jesus spoke to His disciples, all their fears melted into peace. They had rowed and rowed against the wind and waves until fear and fatigue almost plunged them into despair. But when they **willingly** took Him into the boat, **immediately** they were at their destination.

Do you want to reach your destiny in a hurry? Then willingly invite Jesus into your boat. Quit trying to navigate this life with your own compass. Surrender the helm to Him. Your destination is on the other side of some uncharted waters. He alone knows the best route to take. Trust him immediately, without delay, and He will willingly lead you home.

"Father, I'm afraid of the dark. And things always get dark when I try to navigate on my own. I need You to take the helm. Would You hop aboard and take over for me. All this rowing against the wind has worn me out. Thank You, Lord. Amen."

33

How great is the love the Father has lavished on us, that we should be called children of God! — 1 John 3:1 NIV

To lavish means *"to pour forth liberally and bountifully."* Pour is what you do with the Gatorade barrel to the coach after you win the Super Bowl. Pour is what water does over Niagra Falls. You can't pour a drop. The very nature of the word conjures up visions of superabundance, not pittances.

Lavish is what God did with His love when He made us His children. He didn't dab a drop on the back of our ears. He doused us. He backed up His huge dump-truck of grace and love and poured it on us. Lavishly His Son, our Savior, poured His blood out in Pilate's court, Gethsemane and the Cross. He held nothing back. Question is: What are we holding back from Him?

When I coached high school football, we always looked for kids with *reckless abandon* to cover kickoffs. You have to be a little crazy to be on the kickoff team anyway. To be on that team means having only one goal in mind... run as fast as you can and tackle the ball carrier allowing nothing to get in your way. If you get knocked down, you bounce back up barely touching the ground and continue the pursuit. The goal of being the first to get to the ball carrier consumes you.

Nothing else matters. It's only you and the one carrying the ball. Nothing is more important than stopping his progress as soon as possible.

Over the years, I've used the term, *reckless abandon*, to describe how we are to live for Christ. I always thought that God was only pleased with our doing *"God stuff."* You know... witnessing, reading the Bible, praying all the time, studying, preparing sermons, fixing people who needed fixing, doing good spiritual things, and living as holy as possible. Although I still believe those things are good and necessary, I was always analyzing my Christian life. A kickoff team player has no time to analyze. He's too focused on playing the game and his objective... tackle the man with the ball.

After years of study and introspection, I'm coming to realize that I've missed the simplicity of the Gospel. I've made following Jesus far too complicated and analytical. I've discovered that life boils down to this: I need a Savior Who is bigger, stronger and wiser than I am. I can't live pleasing God in my own strength and wisdom. When I cry out to the Lord, all other bets are off. I don't care what kind of sinner I've been, or what I'm involved in be that witchcraft, hedonism or just plain old sin. Once I cry, "God, help me!"... the power of all those things are broken. Jesus came to save us from our sins. We can't do it. Only He can. As long as we think we can overcome the bondage of sin in the energy of the flesh, we will never be free.

Here's the good news. God lavished His love on us when we were still sinners and helplessly trapped by the enemy of our souls. When Jesus died on the Cross, He opened the door of our cage. When we accept by faith His gracious offer of freedom and fly out, He lavishes His love on us again by making us His children.

Now that we are free, what are we free to do? Live. Pure and simple. Jesus said that He came that we might have life and have it more abundantly (John 10:10). Jesus died that we might live. Whenever we live and enjoy the life He gives, Father God is greatly pleased.

Now don't misunderstand me. Don't stop witnessing, praying, or studying the Word, but let me ask you something... why are you doing those things? We study the Word because it is the handbook of living. It shows us how life is to be lived to the max. We pray so that Father's will may be done down here on earth, just like it is being done in heaven. Witnessing takes place while we live and interact with others. We are to be salt and light in this world. Salt can't help my french fries if it stays in the shaker. Light can't help me see if I put it under a blanket.

I'm finding that ministry takes place when I get out there in the world and let it come to me, not when I go out trying to find it. If you decide to live life with reckless abandon, you will find more opportunities to share what you've found in Jesus than you ever will in your ivy-covered tower.

Jesus was the greatest Liver of life there's ever been. He wants to keep on living through you. Stop analyzing Him and start allowing Him to live full and free in you. He's always looking for a few crazy people to run down the field and stop the enemy in his tracks. Go out there today and enjoy life... with reckless abandon!

"Heavenly Father, I'm tired of living life with restraint. You have given me all things to enjoy. You are my Way, my Truth, and my Life. I can make a difference in the world for You and enjoy it at the same time. Today I will live recklessly abandoned to Life. Thank You. Amen."

34

Don't you know that your body is the temple of the Holy Spirit, Who lives in you and was given to you by God? You do not belong to yourself, for God bought you with a high price. So you must honor God with your body.
—1 Corinthians 6:19-20 NLT

Mychal Judge was a New York City Fire Chaplain who was the first official fatality on 9/11. As he ministered to a fallen fireman who had been struck by a falling body, he took off his helmet to pray. As he did, he was struck by debris and killed. On his body was found a prayer that he had written and carried with him for years. It said, *"Lord, take me where You want me to go. Let me meet who You want me to meet. Tell me what You want me to say. And keep me out of Your way."* (*America Out of the Ashes*, Honor Books, 2001, p. 43).

One of the major reasons why we Christians are so miserable is our failure to discern ownership of our lives. When we gave our hearts to Jesus, He not only washed away our sins in His precious blood, He also purchased us with it. We don't belong to ourselves to do whatever we want anymore. We are living on borrowed time. Time that He purchased for us with His Life. We are to live in order to honor God in all we do.

If God loves us perfectly... if He knows what is best for us... if He is absolutely sovereign in wisdom and power, then why do we persist in demanding things go *our* way rather than *His*? We are a selfish lot and extremely short-sighted. Maybe that's why Mychal included in his prayer... *"Lord, keep me out of Your way."*

"Heavenly Father, I know I get in Your way a lot of the time. I'm sorry that I don't trust You more. Would You help me give back to You what is rightfully Yours to begin with. Forgive me for stealing... for taking my life from You and living for my honor rather than Yours. Today, take me where You want to go. Bring people across my path that You want to see today. Put the words in my mouth that You want to say. And please, keep me out of Your way. Thanks for never giving up on me, Lord. Amen."

35

In this is love, not that we loved God, but that He loved us and sent His Son to be the propitiation for our sins.
—1 John 4:10 NKJV

If we are to fulfill our destiny as a soldier of the cross, we must never lose faith in the truth that God is love. Not that God is loving, but that God IS love. It is not merely an attribute of God. Love is His very nature. The world scorns us when we talk of the love of God. The world is filled with selfishness, hatred, bitterness and the pursuit of fleshly pleasure. The world is empty and void of purpose. It pursues its own soulish agendas and has no eternal perspective. It cares not one bit for anyone other than self. That is the spirit of this world.

Nevertheless, God so loved the world that He gave His only begotten Son. Jesus became the "propitiation" for our sins. Propitiation means, "the act of appeasing or making favorable." From the sound of that definition, it seems like God was mad as fire over having to allow His Son to die for us and had to be appeased. God is just as holy as He is love. God's holy nature could not be compromised by our sin. Jesus' death appeased the holiness of God.

Let me illustrate it for you. Suppose a loved one of yours was brutally murdered. Another person comes along and dies in the place of the murderer for his heinous crime. The murderer is forgiven and set free. However, even though someone else paid the penalty, you are probably still real ticked off at the murderer. Right? We tend to have the mistaken impression that God sent His Son to die in our place, but He's still real ticked off that we were the ones who caused Him to die. That's not true at all. God has no harsh feelings toward His children who have by faith trusted in the atoning death of Christ. God is love, and love keeps no record of wrongs (I Corinthians 13:5 NLT). We hold grudges. God is not like us. Imagine that!

Christ's propitiation for our sins not only fulfilled the holy demands of a perfect God but took away any resentment over that fact that Jesus had to die in our place. God is on our side. He is constantly and perpetually pulling for us. We must never forget this truth else when the battle intensifies, we grow weary and lay our weapons down. It happens to the best of us.

Jesus said of John the Baptist that of all men born of women, there was no one greater (Matthew 11:11). When John first saw Jesus, He said, *"Behold the Lamb of God that takes away the sin of the world!"* (John 1:29). John knew Jesus was the Messiah, the Son of God. However, when John was thrown into prison and about to die, John said to his disciples, *"Go and ask Jesus if He is the One, or should we look for another"* (Luke 7:19). When the battle rages, it is easy to lose sight of the truth. One truth we absolutely cannot forget if we are to stand victoriously in His victory is this... God is love. He loves us perfectly whatever our circumstances say to the contrary.

Beloved, Father God loves you. He allows nothing to touch you except those things that are for our ultimate good and for His glory. This is love... not that we loved God, but that He loved us and gave His Son to die in our place so that we can live forever. Oh, what a Savior!

"*Heavenly Father, please give me the grace to always remember how much You love me. I forget far too easily when the battle gets a little hot, and I'm wounded by the shrapnel of the enemy. Remind me that nothing can separate me from Your love. **'Death can't, and life can't. The angels can't, and the demons can't. Our fears for today, our worries about tomorrow, and even the powers of hell can't keep God's love away. Whether we are high above the sky or in the deepest ocean, nothing in all creation will ever be able to separate us from the love of God that is revealed in Christ Jesus our Lord'** (Romans 8:38-39 NLT). Bless the Lord, O my soul, and all that is within me bless Your holy Name! Amen.*"

36

And David was greatly distressed; for the people spake of stoning him, because the soul of all the people was grieved, every man for his sons and for his daughters: but David encouraged himself in the LORD his God.
—1 Samuel 30:6 KJV

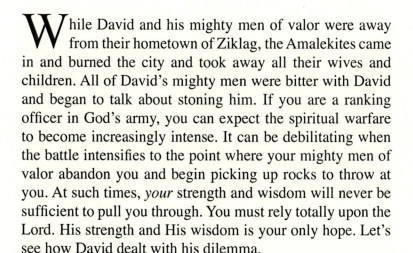

While David and his mighty men of valor were away from their hometown of Ziklag, the Amalekites came in and burned the city and took away all their wives and children. All of David's mighty men were bitter with David and began to talk about stoning him. If you are a ranking officer in God's army, you can expect the spiritual warfare to become increasingly intense. It can be debilitating when the battle intensifies to the point where your mighty men of valor abandon you and begin picking up rocks to throw at you. At such times, *your* strength and wisdom will never be sufficient to pull you through. You must rely totally upon the Lord. His strength and His wisdom is your only hope. Let's see how David dealt with his dilemma.

"But David found strength in the LORD his God. Then he said to Abiathar the priest, 'Bring me the ephod!' So Abiathar brought it. Then David asked the LORD, 'Should I chase them? Will I catch them?' And the LORD told him,

'Yes, go after them. You will surely recover everything that was taken from you!' (1 Samuel 30:6-9 NLT). Strategic ministry implies that we must have a plan... a strategy. Our plans are insufficient. His plans are infallible. The first thing David did was seek the Lord. How simple and yet how profound.

When David got a word and clear direction from the Lord and boldly acted upon His instruction, those same "rock throwers" followed their beleaguered leader into battle and recovered what the enemy had stolen from them. *"David and his men rushed in among them and slaughtered them throughout that night and the entire next day until evening. None of the Amalekites escaped except four hundred young men who fled on camels. David got back everything the Amalekites had taken, and he rescued his two wives. Nothing was missing: small or great, son or daughter, nor anything else that had been taken. David brought everything back. His troops rounded up all the flocks and herds and drove them on ahead. "These all belong to David as his reward!" they said* (1 Samuel 30:17-20 NLT).

"When a man's ways please the LORD, he makes even his enemies to be at peace with him" (Prov 16:7 KJV). We must remember that the enemy's main strategy is to divide and conquer by breeding suspicion, doubt and confusion. Loyal friends can appear to be enemies when clouds of fear and doubt surround them. Great leaders will still love them and carry out the Lord's orders without reservation trusting in His strength and wisdom while despising his own.

It gets lonely in leadership at times, but that's the price as well as the privilege of being entrusted with such a grand blessing as being an officer in the Lord's army. *"A true leader has the confidence to stand alone, the courage to make tough decisions, and the compassion to listen to the needs of others. He does not set out to be a leader, but becomes one by the quality of his actions and the integrity of his intent. In the end, leaders are much like eagles... they don't flock, you find them one at a time"* (source of quote unknown).

Mighty warrior, if you find yourself today in dire straits and no one around who understands or cares, encourage yourself in the Lord. He knows, and He cares. In the final analysis, that's all that really matters.

"Heavenly Father, when no one else understands me, or even cares, I know You do. I am never alone for You are with me. Your rod and Your staff, they comfort me. You are the wind beneath my wings and the lifter of my head. You are my Savior, my Lord, my Friend. The battle is not mine, but Yours. Thanks for the rest. Amen."

37

No matter what happens, always be thankful, for this is God's will for you who belong to Christ Jesus.
—1 Thessalonians 5:18 NLT

∼

We watched a documentary last night about two brothers who suffered from retinitis pigmentosa, a degenerative eye disorder which gradually leads to blindness. The twins inherited the disorder from their mother who went blind at the age of forty. Both were candidates for a new surgical procedure to restore their sight. One brother's sight improved. The other brother's sight did not. Both said that they wanted the other one to have sight if only one could have a successful treatment. It was bittersweet for the sightless brother. The blind brother rejoiced with his sighted brother, but the disappointment of unfulfilled dreams of seeing again produced a curious mixture of joy mingled with sorrow.

I cried as I watched the program. Not long ago, I was lifting some heavy tiles into the trunk of our car when I tore the retina in my right eye. I felt the pressure, but no pain to speak of. Immediately I began to see massive "floaters"... those squiggly looking curly things that float in the vitreous humor of the eye. I had seen floaters for years, but this time was different. I didn't think much about it for a couple of weeks. Then on a Friday afternoon about 3 p.m., the Lord prompted me to call Dr. Bridges, my optometrist. It's almost impossible to talk with her on the phone, but this time she was available. I explained my situation, and she related to me that someone had just canceled an appointment and told me to come to the office right then.

She took a long time to examine my eye. I knew that was not a good sign. She said she had some bad news. My retina had been badly damaged and was on the verge of detaching. My heart jumped into my throat. Blindness is what happens to other people, not me.

If I was ever skeptical that God cared about every detail of my life, it was forever dispelled by what happened next. Dr. Bridges said that Dr. Bonfield, the retinal specialist, had left for the day, but she would check to see for sure. In just a few minutes, she returned with Dr. Bonfield who was in the parking lot preparing to leave. When Dr. Bonfield examined my eye, he was amazed. He had never seen a retinal tear like mine. He said that I was extremely lucky. I don't believe in luck. I believe in the sovereignty of God.

He treated the tear with laser surgery right then and there. According to him, if I had not caught him that day, the retina would have detached over the weekend. I don't even want to go there. Today, I still have some floaters due to the spilling out of blood and pigmentation behind the retina when it tore. Other than that, I can see fine.

Do you realize all the circumstances that God had to orchestrate in order to preserve my sight? I am so thankful. As I sat there and watched the documentary, I couldn't help sympathizing with the sightless brother. That could well have been me. Why did God spare me from blindness and not him? I was overwhelmed with both gratitude and guilt. I take so much for granted. I can see to write this story. I can see my Bride's beautiful face, the brilliant hues of a summer sunset, the facial expressions of people I meet, the break in a 10 foot putt, and the list goes on and on.

The Thessalonians were suffering intense persecution. Paul told them that no matter what happened, they must always be thankful for all things because whatever happened was in God's will and plan for them. I have found that it is easier to give thanks when the results fall in my favor. Would I have been just as thankful had I lost sight in my right eye? Would I have praised Him that I still had one good eye? It all depends upon how much I depend upon His grace. His grace is more than sufficient, but I have to choose whether or not I'll draw upon it. God gives me grace when I thank Him... no matter what happens.

Tearing my retina was a scary thing, but what a boost for my attitude of gratitude. I thank God all the time now. I ask Him for grace to never take Him, or any of His blessings for granted again. He never tires of hearing us say... *"Thank You, Lord, for..."* Now may be a good time to count your blessings and to give thanks.

"Heavenly Father, I'm filled up right now with mixed emotions. I am so blessed. How You must tire of hearing all my gripes and complaints. Lord, forgive me. I am so ungrateful. Paul encouraged the Thessalonians with the hope of Your return when You will make all things right. No matter what happens to me this day, one day You will straighten everything out. In the meantime, I want to thank You for all the things You have given me to enjoy. Give me grace now to constantly abide in an attitude of gratitude come what may. You always know what's best for me. Therefore, I leave the choice up to You as to the course of my life. I'll just be thankful for whatever You decide. Okay with You? Amen."

38

*Now may the God of peace Himself sanctify you
completely; and may your whole spirit, soul, and body
be preserved blameless at the coming of our Lord Jesus
Christ. He who calls you is faithful, Who also will do it.*
— 1 Thessalonians 5:23-24 NKJV

Robert Murray McCheyne, a Scottish minister who lived only 30 years but left a profound impact on Scotland, once prayed... *"Lord, make me as holy as Thou canst make a sinner saved by grace."* Are we prepared to pray that prayer along with Murray?

Sanctification means "a setting apart for God's purposes." Whatever God sets apart for His purpose is considered holy. No one is allowed to touch that which is holy except by God's consent. If we have been made holy through the blood of Christ, then we have no right to ourselves. ***"Do you not know that your body is the temple of the Holy Spirit Who is in you, Whom you have from God, and you are not your own? For you were bought at a price; therefore glorify God in your body and in your spirit, which are God's"*** (1 Cor 6:19-20 NKJV).

Sanctification is a process. We will never be perfect on this side of heaven; therefore, the God of peace will be continually setting us apart until we see Jesus face to face even though we have been made perfect already by the Cross of Christ. ***"For by that one offering He perfected forever all*** *those whom He is making holy"* (Hebrews 10:14 NLT). Do you see that? *He* is making us holy... sanctified... set apart. Father God even sanctified His Son, Jesus. *"Do you say of Him Whom the Father sanctified and sent into the world, 'You are blaspheming,' because I said, 'I am the Son of God'"?* (John 10:36-37 NKJV). But even though Father God sanctified our Lord, Jesus also sanctified Himself as well. *"And for their sakes I sanctify Myself, that they also may be sanctified by the truth"* (John 17:19 NKJV). Even though God Himself is sanctifying us, we have the choice of either cooperating with Him, or opposing Him.

Are we prepared for what sanctification will cost us? Are we willing to give up all our interests for what interests the Lord? Are we willing to give up our point of view, our agenda for God's? Do we realize that sanctification will cost us everything that is not God in us? Are we willing to let the Holy Spirit put us under His microscope and cut out every minute particle that stands in opposition to Him?

God is holy. He wants us to be wholly devoted to Him. Sanctification begins the minute we let go and let God. Are you ready?

"Heavenly Father, I want to be set apart for You and You alone. I admit that I don't really know all that is involved, but I do know that I love You and want to love You more. Would You come and remove from me anything that is not of You and make more room for You in me. I am willing, but my flesh becomes weak. If I begin to complain about some of the things You remove, don't pay any attention. Just keep on keeping on until I am Yours wholly and completely. I've tried everything else in the world to fill this emptiness inside of me, but I now know that You are the only One who can fill it totally and completely. Begin the work in me, Lord, and don't stop until all that is within me blesses You. This I pray in the matchless Name of Your Son and my Lord. Amen."

39

No one has ever seen God; but if we love one another, God lives in us and His love is made complete in us.
—1 John 4:12 NIV

~

John Powell, a professor at Loyola University in Chicago writes about a student named Tommy in his Theology of Faith class.

Some twelve years ago, I stood watching my university students file into the classroom for our first session in the Theology of Faith. That was the day I first saw Tommy. My eyes and my mind both blinked. He was combing his long flaxen hair which hung six inches below his shoulders. It was the first time I had ever seen a boy with hair that long. I guess it was just coming into fashion then. I know in my mind that it isn't what's on your head but what's in it that counts; but on that day I was unprepared and my emotions flipped. I immediately filed Tommy under "S" for strange... very strange.

Tommy turned out to be the "atheist in residence" in my Theology of Faith course. He constantly objected to, smirked at, or whined about the possibility of an unconditionally loving Father/God. We lived with each other in relative peace for one semester, although I admit he was, for me at times, a serious pain in the back pew. When he came up at the end of the course to turn in his final exam, he asked in a slightly cynical tone,*"Do you think I'll ever find God?"*

I decided instantly on a little shock therapy. *"No!"* I said very emphatically.

"Oh," he responded, *"I thought that was the product you were pushing."*

I let him get five steps from the classroom door, then called out, *"Tommy! I don't think you'll ever find Him, but I am absolutely certain that He will find you!"* He shrugged a little and left my class and my life. I felt slightly disappointed at the thought that he had missed my clever line: *"He will find you!"* At least I thought it was clever.

Later I heard that Tommy had graduated, and I was duly grateful. Then a sad report came. I heard Tommy had terminal cancer. Before I could search him out, he came to see me. When he walked into my office, his body was very badly wasted, and the long hair had all fallen out as a result of chemotherapy, but his eyes were bright, and his voice was firm for the first time, I believe.

"Tommy, I've thought about you so often. I hear you are sick," I blurted out.

"Oh, yes, very sick. I have cancer in both lungs. It's a matter of weeks."

"Can you talk about it, Tom?" I asked.

"Sure, what would you like to know?" he replied.

"What's it like to be only twenty-four and dying?"

"Well, it could be worse."

"Like what?"

"Well, like being fifty and having no values or ideals; like being fifty and thinking that booze, seducing women, and making money are the real 'biggies' in life." (I began to look through my mental file cabinet under 'S' where I had filed Tommy as strange. It seems as though everybody I try to reject by classification, God sends back into my life to educate me.)

Jesus... My Final Answer

"But what I really came to see you about," Tom said, *"is something you said to me on the last day of class."* (He remembered!) He continued, *"I asked you if you thought I would ever find God, and you said, 'No!' which surprised me. Then you said, 'But He will find you.' I thought about that a lot, even though my search for God was hardly intense at that time."* (My clever line... He thought about that a lot!) *"But when the doctors removed a lump from my groin and told me that it was malignant, that's when I got serious about locating God. And when the malignancy spread into my vital organs, I really began banging bloody fists against the bronze doors of heaven, but God did not come out. In fact, nothing happened. Did you ever try something for a long time with great effort and with no success? You get psychologically glutted; fed up with trying. And then you quit. Well, one day I woke up, and instead of throwing a few more futile appeals over that high brick wall to a God Who may or may not be there, I just quit. I decided that I didn't really care about God, about an afterlife, or anything like that. I decided to spend what time I had left doing something more profitable. I thought about you and your class, and I remembered something else you had said: 'The ultimate sadness is to go through life without loving. But it would be almost equally sad to go through life and leave this world without ever telling those you loved that you had loved them.' So, I began with the hardest one, my Dad. He was reading the newspaper when I approached him."*

"Dad."

"Yes, what?" he asked without lowering the newspaper.

"Dad, I would like to talk with you."

"Well, talk."

"I mean it's really important."

The newspaper came down three slow inches. *"What is it?"*

"*Dad, I love you. I just wanted you to know that.*" (Tom smiled at me and said it with obvious satisfaction, as though he felt a warm and secret joy flowing inside of him.)

"*The newspaper fluttered to the floor. Then my father did two things I could never remember him ever doing before. He cried, and he hugged me. We talked all night, even though he had to go to work the next morning. It felt so good to be close to my father, to see his tears, to feel his hug, to hear him say that he loved me. It was easier with my mother and little brother. They cried with me, too, and we hugged each other, and started saying real nice things to each other. We shared the things we had been keeping secret for so many years. I was only sorry about one thing... that I had waited so long. Here I was, just beginning to open up to all the people I had actually been close to.*"

"*Then, one day, I turned around and God was there! He didn't come to me when I pleaded with Him. I guess I was like an animal trainer holding out a hoop; 'C'mon, jump through. C'mon, I'll give You three days, three weeks.' Apparently God does things in His own way and at His own hour. But the important thing is that He was there. He found me. You were right. He found me even after I stopped looking for Him.*"

"*Tommy,*" I practically gasped, "*I think you are saying something very important and much more universal than you realize. To me, at least, you are saying that the surest way to find God is not to make Him a private possession, a problem solver, or an instant consolation in time of need, but rather to open up to love. You know, the Apostle John said that. He said:* **'God is love, and anyone who lives in love is living with God and God is living in Him.'**"

"*Tom, could I ask you a favor? You know, when I had you in class you were a real pain. But (laughingly) you can make it all up to me now. Would you come into my present Theology of Faith course and tell them what you have just* told me? If I told them the same thing it wouldn't be half as effective as if you were to tell them."

"Oh, I was ready for you, but I don't know if I'm ready for your class."

"Tom, think about it. If and when you are ready, give me a call."

In a few days, Tom called, said he was ready for the class; that he wanted to do that for God and for me. So we scheduled a date, but he never made it. He had another appointment, far more important than the one with me and my class. Of course, his life was not really ended by his death, only changed. He made the great step from faith into vision. He found a life far more beautiful than the eye of man has ever seen or the ear of man has ever heard, or the mind of man has ever imagined.

Before he died, we talked one last time. *"I'm not going to make it to your class,"* he said.

"I know, Tom."

"Will you tell them for me? Will you... tell the whole world for me?"

"I will, Tom. I'll tell them. I'll do my best."

Like Tom, I've been searching for God all my life. I've read the Bible, studied, prayed, witnessed, preached, taught, tried to live right, begged and pleaded with God to be real to me. Then one day a few months ago, I got tired. I gave up hope that God would ever be what I... emphasis on "I"... wanted Him to be. My pursuit of God was like trying to climb Mt. Everest in gym shorts and street shoes. I simply couldn't climb anymore. I gave up... gave in... gave out. Whatever you want to call it. I discovered as did Tom that God is found by loving one another. Not just saying it, but in doing it. I find that God is right there all the time whenever I love people without expecting anything out of them. Life is a gift from God to enjoy and savor. It is not meant to be dissected and studied, but to be lived to the max... every second... every minute.

Beloved, let's not wait until we are about to die before we start to live. God is a Lover, not a tyrant. Maybe we've been looking for Him in all the wrong places. Stop looking and start living and loving, and He will find you.

"Heavenly Father, thanks for not giving up Your search for me. I love You. Amen."

40

They are not of the world, just as I am not of the world.
   —John 17:16 NKJV

Have you ever mulled a bunch of stuff over and over in your mind for a long time and could just never make sense of it all? Then one day, it all just falls together and makes perfect sense because the Lord just comes and sorts it out for you. You know what I mean?

Let me explain. I've been wondering why people in high places of authority can be so intelligent and then act so stupid. Take, for instance, the judges who ruled that "under God" in the Pledge of Allegiance promotes religion and therefore, must be banned. Or a court system which will allow a mother to kill a baby within her womb, while a man who kills a pregnant woman is charged with two counts of murder... the mother and the child. Or if God is the ultimate reality, and people out of touch with reality are considered insane, then why won't mental health facilities allow counselors to even mention the name of God?

Then it dawned on me, the world will never change. The devil is its ruler (Ephesians 6:12). The Greek word for "world" is *kosmos* which means "the system by which the world operates." It is diametrically opposed to God's Kingdom. God's Kingdom will never change and neither will satan's. The reason I have been so frustrated lately is because I have been trying to change the world. If we could just get some Christian Supreme Court Justices... If we could get a Senate with a majority of Christians... If we could get the world to submit to God's principles... then we could turn this world around. The Lord finally got my attention. **"Kenny, it's just not going to happen. I never called you to change the world. I called you to rescue people out of it and train those you rescue how to rescue others. When you give up hope that the world can be changed, you will feel a lot better and a lot less frustrated."**

"For He has rescued us from the one who rules in the kingdom of darkness, and He has brought us into the Kingdom of His dear Son. God has purchased our freedom with His blood and has forgiven all our sins" (Colossians 1:13-14 NLT). Since the Lord Jesus has rescued us, our job is to proclaim the good news to others trapped in the kingdom of darkness. *"For God was in Christ, reconciling the world to Himself, no longer counting people's sins against them. This is the wonderful message He has given us to tell others. We are Christ's ambassadors, and God is using us to speak to you"* (2 Corinthians 5:19-20 NLT).

I no longer watch the news and marvel at how ignorantly the world acts. The world is a kingdom of darkness. Let's not get all bent out of shape over it. Why don't we pray for God's grace to fall upon those trapped in it and light a candle rather than becoming overwhelmed by the darkness. Jesus said, **"You are the light of the world--like a city on a mountain, glowing in the night for all to see. Don't hide your light under a basket! Instead, put it on a stand and let it shine for all. In the same way, let your good deeds shine out for all to see, so that everyone will praise your heavenly Father"** (Matthew 5:14-16 NLT).

I see the world differently today. Could you use a different *world view*?

"*Heavenly Father, You call me the light of the world, but I only reflect You, the true Light. Keep me shiny and clean so that I reflect every ray of Your brilliance so that the world will see how wonderful You truly are. Thanks for rescuing me. Make me a real life-guard for You. Amen.*"

41

And we will be ready to punish every act of disobedience, once your obedience is complete. —2 Corinthians 10:6 NIV

Ever wonder why God doesn't fix your wife, or your husband, or your children, or your boss, or your pastor, or anyone else who may be giving you a hard time? Oh how you have prayed for them, talked with them, corrected them and even preached to them, and they still have not changed one bit. What's the problem?

If we look back a few verses for context, we find... **"For though we live in the world, we do not wage war as the world does. The weapons we fight with are not the weapons of the world. On the contrary, they have divine power to demolish strongholds. We demolish arguments and every pretension that sets itself up against the knowledge of God, and we take captive every thought to make it obedient to Christ"** (2 Corinthians 10:3-5 NIV). A "stronghold" is pattern of thinking that is contrary to God's way of thinking. I call it "stinking thinking." We all have strongholds to a certain extent. That's why Paul beseeches us not to be conformed to this world, but to be transformed by the renewing of our minds (Romans 12:2). Renewing our minds to think like God thinks is called, "repentance." The root of that word means "to think." The prefix "re" means "back, or from." Repentance basically means "to think in the opposite direction." Right thinking is high on God's list of priorities because *"as a man thinks in his heart, so is he"* (Proverbs 23:7 KJV).

God wants to tear down our strongholds. He's the only one Who can. He wants us to utilize the mind of Christ which He has given us as children of God, but our way of thinking often gets in God's way. Instead of repenting and lining up with what God thinks, we usually try to change the people and circumstances around us. We forget that God did not save us to fix other people. That's His job.

The reason we cannot fix these people and rearrange our circumstances is because God is using them to make us aware of our own strongholds so that we will come to Him to demolish them. God wants unconditional surrender of our lives to Him. Nothing else will satisfy Him. Are you willing to surrender absolute control of your life to the Lord? Before you answer, would you be willing to completely obey the Lord even if He not only refused to change those aggravating people and circumstances but made them even worse? Do you trust in the character and integrity of the Lord? Does He love you perfectly? Did He die in your place while you were still a sinner? How could you not trust a God like that? Simple. You have a stronghold that demands that you be in control rather than the Lord. In essence, you trust in yourself more than God. What does the Lord think of that? *"Cursed is the man who trusts in man and makes flesh his strength, whose heart departs from the LORD. For he shall be like a shrub in the desert, and shall not see when good comes, but shall inhabit the parched places in the wilderness, in a salt land which is not inhabited"* (Jeremiah 17:5-6 NKJV). Kinda scary, isn't it?

By now, you are probably thinking... *"Doesn't God want those pesky people that keep hassling me to change, too?"* Of course, He does, but He is getting a lot of mileage out of them. He is using them to rub off your rough edges to bring you to the point of surrender to Him. When His purpose for them is accomplished in your life, then God will be free to change them as well. He will punish every disobedience in their lives, when your obedience is complete. That is, when you give God what He wants, it frees Him up to give you what you want. However, there is one thing I've discovered. When I give God what He wants, He changes me so that it doesn't really matter anymore if I get what I want, or if all those aggravating people and circumstances get fixed.

I wonder why I hold on so strongly when He's waiting patiently to hold me so securely.

"Heavenly Father, change me. Forgive me for always asking you to give to me. What I really need is for You to change me into Your image. Don't give up on me, Lord. Please. Amen."

42

Now go out and encourage your men. I swear by the LORD that if you don't go out, not a man will be left with you by nightfall. —2 Samuel 19:6 NIV

Billy came bursting in the door from Kindergarten one day and proudly announced to his mom, *"Mom, Joe said I was the best baseball player in the whole class!"* Of course Mom concurred and added her own accolades about his athletic ability. After a moment of reflection, Billy turned to his mom, *"You know, Mom, Joe is my best friend."*

What the world needs now is encouragement... sweet encouragement. One of satan's most devastating tools is discouragement. If he can get us to lose heart, then he has us whipped.

Our Scripture for today finds David grieving over the death of his son, Absalom, who rebelled against his dad and tried to steal his kingdom. The king's mighty men of valor risked life and limb to save David, his family and his kingdom, and all he can do is put his head between his legs and cry. Joab, the commander of David's mighty men, rebukes the king. **Then Joab went into the house to the king and said, "Today you have humiliated all your men, who have just saved your life and the lives of your sons and daughters and the lives of your wives and concubines. You** *love those who hate you and hate those who love you. You have made it clear today that the commanders and their men mean nothing to you. I see that you would be pleased if Absalom were alive today and all of us were dead. Now go out and encourage your men. I swear by the LORD that if you don't go out, not a man will be left with you by nightfall. This will be worse for you than all the calamities that have come upon you from your youth till now"* (2 Samuel 19:5-7 NIV).

We cannot make it without encouragement. The world and the devil are out to steal our joy and destroy our lives. Without an encouraging word now and then, the enemies of our soul would surely overwhelm us. Will Rogers used to say that he could live two weeks on a good compliment.

If encouragement is so vital to our well-being, and if it is so easy to do, then why don't we do more of it? You tell me. Maybe we are so self-absorbed that we don't think about it. Or maybe we are so bent on seeking encouragement for ourselves that we don't have time to give it. Well, far be it from me not to practice what I preach. I don't want to be accused of giving flowers to the dead who can't enjoy them. I want to give a couple of roses of encouragement right now.

There are two ladies in our church family that have encouraged me at times when no one else would. They have been like that first breath of air after almost going down for the third time. Connie and Marilyn are two of the sweetest, nicest, most pleasant people I've ever known. They never have anything negative to say about anyone and can find something good to say about everyone. When I leave their presence, the spring in my step is a little bit livelier, my head is lifted a little higher, and my confidence soars. They are simply the best.

Those ladies think nothing about it. They don't set out to do it. It's just their nature. They are like wind beneath my wings. And I love them for it. They make me feel best about me when I'm around them. What a blessing they are. How we need more of them. May their tribe increase!

As great as Connie and Marilyn are, there is none better at this encouraging thing than Jesus. He believes in us at our worst. He still pulls for us when we are behind, loves us when we are unlovable, and never says, *"I told you so"* even though He's told us so a hundred times. He is faithful when we are unfaithful, cares for us when we don't care, walks in when everyone else walks out, and thinks we can when we know we can't. What a Friend!

You know what? Jesus is my best Friend. I want to be just like Him. Don't you?

"Lord Jesus, I do feel best about me when I'm around You. Would You encourage others through me today so that I can help them feel best about themselves when they're around You and me? Thanks. Amen."

43

If you keep yourself pure, you will be a utensil God can use for His purpose. Your life will be clean, and you will be ready for the Master to use you for every good work.
—2 Timothy 2:20-21 NLT

Do you have a favorite chair? A favorite cup? A favorite room? It is your favorite because it gives you pleasure, right? Today, the Lord reminded me that He created everything, and it is for His pleasure that they exist and were created" (Revelation 4:11 NLT). Favorite things are given honor by the use made of them by the owner.

I know a young man named Mark whose pet saying is, *"I'm God's favorite."* We joke with him about his modesty, but I think he's right. The Lord did purchase us at great cost. **"Don't you know that your body is the temple of the Holy Spirit, Who lives in you and was given to you by God? You do not belong to yourself, for God bought you with a high price"** (1 Cor 6:19-20 NLT). You can always tell how much something is worth by how much it costs. You and I were bought with the very blood of Christ. You may not think as much of yourself as Mark, but Jesus certainly does.

A cup cannot scratch your back, mow your lawn or drive you into town, but when you want something to drink, it's perfect. It was created to give pleasure to the one who drinks from it. Do you drink from it all the time? No, but when you do, it gives you great pleasure. The cup's only responsibility is to remain available for its owner and to stay true to the purpose for which it was created. So it is with you... God's favorite. Your only responsibility is to always be available for the Master's use and refrain from trying to be something you're not.

Beloved, God created you just the way He wanted you. Nobody can do what you do. You are an unique, precious creation with a tailor-made array of gifts, talents and abilities like no other person in the universe. You are, indeed, God's favorite. You give Him great pleasure whenever You allow Him to use You for the very purpose for which He created you.

Keep yourself pure. Don't dilute yourself by trying to be all things to all people. Don't beat yourself up because you are not gifted in certain areas. Remember that a jack-of-all-trades is a master of none. God created you to be a master of a specific purpose. Stay true to the Master's design. When He wants to use you, make sure you are clean and ready for use. Take delight in the fact that you are God's favorite. Enjoy His enjoyment today.

"Heavenly Father, it thrills my heart that I'm Your favorite. I cannot do everything, but then You didn't create me or expect me to do everything. The things that I can do, I do excellently because You empower me to do so. I want to be available to You today, Lord. Whenever You need me, I'm here. Just let me know. Help me to celebrate other people's gifts and abilities rather than covet them. Keep me pure and clean and ready for You today. Amen."

44

For they have deserted Me and turned to worthless idols. They have stumbled off the ancient highways of good, and they walk the muddy paths of sin. Therefore, their land will become desolate, a monument to their stupidity. All who pass by will be astonished and shake their heads in amazement at its utter desolation.
—Jeremiah 18:15-16 NLT

One evening a grandson was talking to his grandmother about current events. The grandson asked his grandmother what she thought about the shootings at schools, the computer age, and just things in general.

The Grandma replied...

"Well, let me think a minute, I was born, before television, penicillin, polio shots, frozen foods, Xerox, contact lenses, Frisbees and the pill. There was no radar, credit cards, laser beams or ball-point pens. Man had not invented pantyhose, air conditioners, dishwashers, clothes dryers, and the clothes were hung out to dry in the fresh air and man hadn't yet walked on the moon. Your Grandfather and I got married first-and then lived together. Every family had a father and a mother. Until I was 25, I called every man older than I, 'Sir'- and after I turned 25, I still called policemen and every man with a title, 'Sir.' We were before gay-rights, computer-dating, dual careers, daycare centers, and group therapy. Our lives were governed by the Ten Commandments, good judgment, and common sense. We were taught to know the difference between right and wrong and to stand up and take responsibility for our actions. Serving your country was a privilege; living in this country was a bigger privilege. We thought fast food was what people ate during Lent. Having a meaningful relationship meant getting along with your cousins. Draft dodgers were people who closed their front doors when the evening breeze started. Time-sharing meant time the family spent together in the evenings and weekends — not purchasing condominiums. We never heard of FM radios, tape decks, CD's, electric typewriters, yogurt, or guys wearing earrings. We listened to the Big Bands, Jack Benny, and the President's speeches on our radios. And I don't ever remember a kid blowing his brains out listening to Tommy Dorsey. If you saw anything with 'Made in Japan' on it, it was junk. The term 'making out' referred to how you did on your school exam. Pizza Hut, McDonald's, and instant coffee were unheard of. We had 5 & 10-cent stores where you could actually buy things for 5 and 10 cents. Ice-cream cones, phone calls, rides on a streetcar, and a Pepsi were all a nickel. And if you didn't want to splurge, you could spend your nickel on enough stamps to mail 1 letter and 2 postcards. You could buy a new Chevy Coupe for $600 but who could afford one? Too bad, because gas was 11 cents a gallon. In my day, "grass" was mowed, "coke" was a cold drink, "pot" was something your mother cooked in, and "rock music" was your grandmother's lullaby. "Aids" were helpers in the Principal's office, "chip" meant a piece of wood, "hardware" was found in a hardware store, and "software" wasn't even a word. And we were the last generation to actually believe that a lady needed a husband to have a baby. No wonder people call us 'old and confused' and say there is a generation gap." (source unknown)

How old do you really think this grandma is? This woman is only 58 years old! Pretty scary if you think about it and pretty sad at the same time.

The Ancient Highways are not that ancient after all, are they?

"Father, thanks for the reminder that good morals, integrity and wholesomeness are always in fashion. Don't let them die out in generations to come. May I pass the torch and may all who come behind me find me faithful. May the fire of my devotion to You and Your value system light their way. Amen."

45

At my first defense, no one came to my support, but everyone deserted me. May it not be held against them. But the Lord stood at my side and gave me strength...
—2 Timothy 4:16-17 NIV

When Jesus fulfilled His ultimate act of obedience, the Cross, He was all alone. Everyone deserted Him. He even thought His Father deserted Him and turned His back on Him. I used to think Father God turned His back while Jesus paid for our sins, but the Holy Spirit enlightened me about that. The Lord Jesus, the sinless One, was made sin for us. **"God made Him who had no sin to be sin for us, so that in Him we might become the righteousness of God"** (2 Corinthians 5:20-21 NIV). Isaiah tells us... **"All we like sheep have gone astray; we have turned every one to his own way; and the LORD hath laid on Him the iniquity of us all"** (Isa 53:6 KJV). **"Your iniquities have separated you from your God; your sins have hidden his face from you"** (Isaiah 59:2 NIV). Sin separates us from God. We lose sight of Him and our intimacy with Him is destroyed whenever we sin. When Jesus became sin for us, Father God's face was hidden from Him. Because our sin blinded Jesus, the Son of Man thought His Father had forsaken Him.

Father had not turned away, but Jesus perceived that He had. Perception is reality. When Jesus paid our sin debt, He felt totally alone... abandoned... forsaken. It had to be. Why? *"This High Priest of ours understands our weaknesses, for He faced all of the same temptations we do, yet He did not sin"* (Hebrews 4:14-16 NLT). How could Jesus understand my loneliness if He had never experienced it? Jesus knows like no other what it means to be totally alone. There is no pain like loneliness. Whenever you feel like no one is there, or cares, the fear and agony is unbearable. Jesus knows. That's why He says... **"I will not in any way fail you nor give you up nor leave you without support. I will not, I will not, I will not in any degree leave you helpless nor forsake you nor let you down [relax My hold on you!] Assuredly not!"** (Hebrews 13:5 AMP). To put it in layman's terms... He ain't gonna leave!

The servant is not greater than His Master. If we are to glorify Christ, we will be called upon to stand alone just as He did. However, because of the Cross, we never really stand alone even when everyone else deserts us. He is always standing with us... faithful and true to the end. If Jesus is to be our Final Answer, then God must bring us to the realization that He is our Only Answer. If we are depending on anyone else for what He alone can supply, then God will remove those people from our lives. We have a tendency to make idols out of people. An idol is anyone or anything we trust to meet our needs other than God. God says that He will have no other gods before Him. They all must go.

Early on in our walk with Christ, disillusionment is inevitable. People we thought were lights will flicker out and those who used to stand with us will pass away. God wants to get us to the place where when we stand alone we are not even aware that we are alone. People come and go, but the Lord stands strong by our side. When God removes people we thought we couldn't live without, we are sad until we realize that they were meant to go. *"They went out from us, but they did not really belong to us. For if they had belonged to us, they would have remained with us; but their going showed that none of them belonged to us"* (1 John 2:18-19 NIV).

Beloved, don't build your life on lights that will fade. Walk and trust in the Light that shines ever brighter until the full light of day. You are never alone.

"Heavenly Father, You are the Light of my life. Forgive me for trusting in lesser lights. Grant me the grace and courage to walk alone with You so that I never know I'm alone even when no one is around. You are faithful and true. I love You so much. Thank You, Lord. Amen."

46

And no doubt you know that God anointed Jesus of Nazareth with the Holy Spirit and with power. Then Jesus went around doing good... —Acts 10:38 NLT

I've been thinking a lot lately about why we are here on this planet. If God wanted fellowship with us, why didn't He just keep us up there in heaven with Him? What purpose does God have for us anyway? Is it to become theologians so we can expound upon the unsearchable mysteries of God? Why do we have Bible studies? Why do we go to church? Why do we memorize Scripture? Why do we do what we do in what we call church?

We live in a dark fallen world that desperately needs some light. We live in a world that is morally decaying by the minute that desperately needs a preservative to prevent it from rotting completely. Jesus called us to be light and salt. Light helps people see how to walk in a dark world without getting hurt or hurting others. Salt preserves, prevents decay and makes you thirsty. How do we do that? I don't think we do it sitting around talking about it. We do it by lighting one candle instead of cursing the darkness. We do it by not rubbing salt into the wounds of hurting people, but by making them thirsty for the love and peace we have in Jesus. In a word... we love people to life just like Jesus loved us.

Jesus... My Final Answer

We do that by smiling instead of frowning... by encouraging rather than criticizing... by blessing instead of cursing... by doing good instead of doing nothing.

I'm reminded of a story. I don't know who wrote it, but it illustrates the point I'm trying to make.

During the waning years of the depression in a small southeastern Idaho community, I used to stop by Mr. Miller's roadside stand for farm-fresh produce as the season made it available. Food and money were still extremely scarce and bartering was used extensively. One particular day, Mr. Miller was bagging some early potatoes for me. I noticed a small boy, delicate of bone and feature, ragged but clean, hungrily apprizing a basket of freshly picked green peas. I paid for my potatoes but was also drawn to the display of fresh green peas. I am a pushover for creamed peas and new potatoes. Pondering the peas, I couldn't help overhearing the conversation between Mr. Miller and the ragged boy next to me.

"Hello Barry, how are you today?"

"H'lo, Mr. Miller. Fine, thank ya. Jus' admirin' them peas... sure look good."

"They are good, Barry. How's your Ma?"

"Fine. Gittin' stronger alla' time."

"Good. Anything I can help you with?"

"No, Sir. Jus' admirin' them peas."

"Would you like to take some home?"

"No, Sir. Got nuthin' to pay for 'em with."

"Well, what have you to trade me for some of those peas?"

"All I got's my prize marble here."

"Is that right? Let me see it."

"Here 'tis. She's a dandy."

"I can see that. Hmmmm, only thing is this one is blue, and I sort of go for red. Do you have a red one like this at home?"

"Not 'zackley ... but, almost."

"Tell you what. Take this sack of peas home with you and next trip this way let me look at that red marble."
"Sure will. Thanks, Mr. Miller."

Mrs. Miller, who had been standing nearby, came over to help me. With a smile she said: *"There are two other boys like him in our community. All three are in very poor circumstances. Jim just loves to bargain with them for peas, apples, tomatoes or whatever. When they come back with their red marbles, and they always do, he decides he doesn't like red after all. Then he sends them home with a bag of produce for a green marble or perhaps an orange one."* Smiling to myself, I left the stand impressed with this man.

A short time later I moved to Colorado, but I never forgot the story of this man, the boys and their bartering. Several years went by each more rapid than the previous one. Just recently I had occasion to visit some old friends in that Idaho community. While I was there, I learned that Mr. Miller had died. They were having his viewing that evening and knowing my friends wanted to go, I agreed to accompany them.

Upon our arrival at the mortuary we fell into line to meet the relatives of the deceased and to offer whatever words of comfort we could. Ahead of us in line were three young men. One was in an army uniform and the other two wore nice haircuts, dark suits and white shirts... very professional looking. They approached Mrs. Miller standing smiling and composed by her husband's casket. Each of the young men hugged her, kissed her on the cheek, spoke briefly with her and moved on to the casket. Her misty light blue eyes followed them as, one by one, each young man stopped briefly and placed his own warm hand over the cold pale hand in the casket. Each left the mortuary awkwardly wiping his eyes.

Our turn came to meet Mrs. Miller. I told her who I was and mentioned the story she had told me about the marbles. Eyes glistening she took my hand and led me to the casket.

Jesus... My Final Answer

"Those three young men who just left were the boys I told you about. They just told me how they appreciated the things Jim 'traded' them. Now at last when Jim could not change his mind about color or size, they came to pay their debt. We've never had a great deal of the wealth of this world," she confided, "but right now, Jim would consider himself the richest man in Idaho." With loving gentleness she lifted the lifeless fingers of her deceased husband. Resting underneath were three, exquisitely shined red marbles.

Beloved, we will not be remembered by our words, but by our kind deeds. Life is not measured by the breaths we take but by the moments that take our breath. God Loves You. Today, I pray for you to know that from the top of your head to the soles of your feet. I pray for you a day of ordinary miracles... a fresh pot of coffee you didn't make yourself... an unexpected phone call from an old friend... green stoplights on your way to work or shop. I pray for you a day of little things to rejoice in... the fastest line at the grocery store... a good sing along song on the radio... your keys right where you look. I pray for you a day of happiness and perfection... little bite-size pieces of perfection that give you the funny feeling that the Lord is smiling on you, holding you so gently because you are someone special and rare. I pray for you a day of peace, happiness and joy.

They say it takes a minute to find a special person, an hour to appreciate them, a day to love them, but then an entire lifetime to forget them. Special people make all their marbles count. Trade yours wisely today.

"Heavenly Father, my life is too complicated. I'm tired of learning about You. Today, I just want to be with You. Please don't let me run by life in my pursuit of what I think will make me happy. I'm learning that I'm happier when I'm making other people happy. Simplify my life this day. Make all my marbles count. Take my breath away... moment by moment. I love You, too. Amen."

47

Giving thanks always for all things unto God and the Father in the name of our Lord Jesus Christ.
—Ephesians 5:20 KJV

Miss Bertha Smith, the great Southern Baptist missionary to China, believed that this verse was the key to abundant life. I think she was right. Our altitude is determined by our attitude, and our attitude must be first and foremost one of gratitude.

We thank God for everything not because we *feel* thankful, but because we trust in the sovereignty of Almighty God who works ALL things together for our good. Every circumstance that touches our lives has to pass before the Lord before it ever reaches us. God has a redemptive purpose for everything that happens to us.

We don't necessarily feel like thanking God when our dog dies, or we lose our job, or we get our feelings hurt, but we thank Him because He has a plan... a plan to prosper us and give us a future and a hope (Jeremiah 29:11). No, we can't see what all God is up to when bad things happen, but we can rest in the fact that He does. When we thank Him in all things, we bless His heart with our dependence and trust.

We are not nearly thankful enough. We take so much for granted until we lose it. Whenever the power goes off in a storm, do you still keep turning on light switches to no avail? See what I mean? We take so much for granted. When is the last time you thanked Him for your eyesight, your hearing, your health, the feel of a warm shower, the colors of autumn, the beauty of a cloudless sky, your car that cranked right away and carried you to your destination, the scrumptious taste of strawberry ice cream on a sugar cone, a child's embrace, butterfly kisses... You fill in the rest.

According to the Word of God, everyday... every minute is supposed to be a time of thanksgiving. Why not start now?

"Thank You, Father, for this reminder. Keep me in an attitude of gratitude today. Amen."

48

Then the LORD asked him, "What do you have there in your hand?" —Exodus 4:2 NLT

In Exodus chapter four, Moses encounters God at the burning bush. God called Moses to lead His children out of Egypt. Moses gave Him every excuse in the book in an effort to make God realize that He had the wrong man. *"Who am I that the elders of Israel and Pharaoh will believe me. Besides, I can't speak very well. And I know they will ask me Who sent me. Then what will I tell them?"*

Then God goes on to tell Him what to say and do and that He will protect and deliver him and all the children of Israel. All Moses had to do was go and listen to the Lord on the way. He would tell Moses everything he needed to do and say. But Moses still was not convinced.

Then the LORD asked him, "What do you have there in your hand?"
"A shepherd's staff," Moses replied.
"Throw it down on the ground," *the LORD told him. So Moses threw it down, and it became a snake! Moses was terrified, so he turned and ran away.* (Exodus 4:2-3 NLT).

What Moses feared the most was having a job description but no authority to pull it off. God gave him an object lesson. Moses staff represented his authority over his little flock of sheep. But that staff was full of Moses and his authority, beliefs and agendas. Before God could use this unlikely deliverer, Moses needed to have a "white funeral" as Oswald Chambers calls it. Moses had to die to all that was not of God's purposes and agenda. Moses throwing down his staff symbolized a surrender of self to God's sovereignty. What Moses saw in himself, as represented by his staff turning into a snake, scared him to death.

God took Moses out of the equation and substituted His authority and might. **Then the LORD told him, "Take hold of its tail."** *So Moses reached out and grabbed it, and it became a shepherd's staff again* (Exodus 4:4 NLT). Having taken the snake out (Moses faulty belief system and self-trust), God exercised His mighty power and authority through that staff in Moses' hand to overcome the Egyptians and deliver His children.

It's a funny thing. Moses was right. He was worthless, no good, ungifted. However, that's the only people God can use. Our gifts, talents and abilities more often than not become a hindrance to God's utilization of us for His purposes. We trust more in our strength than we do in God's. That's why the Lord keeps putting us in situations that we can't handle on our own. When we finally see that *"cursed is the person who trusts in the flesh and makes the arm of flesh His strength"* (Jeremiah 17:5), it scares us to death, too. Many run away from God when they see themselves. Many are still running, but there is no where to run. Sooner or later we will run out of our own strength and be right back at the same place... exhausted and hopeless. No matter how gifted, talented and blessed we are, we are nothing without Him.

The Lord is asking you to throw down your life. Quit trusting in yourself. Abandon your agenda and let God remove the snake. That old serpent, the devil, will always try to get you to trust in your abilities and strength rather than God. Don't listen to him. Let the Lord crush his ugly head. He will give you your staff, your gifts, your talents and your abilities back to you, but He will first transform them into instruments of righteousness so that they can to be used for His glory.

Beloved, what's that in *your* hand?

"Father, all I have in my hand, I throw down... my abilities, my gifts, my talents, my self-sufficiency. I am nothing without You, Lord, and all that I have I received from You. I don't like what I see in me. Transform me into Your image. I want to think what You think, feel what You feel, see what You see. Live Your life through me today. Amen."

49

Think of ways to encourage one another to outbursts of love and good deeds. —Hebrews 10:24 NLT

Some of the greatest success stories of history have followed a word of encouragement or an act of confidence by a loved one or a trusting friend. Had it not been for a confident wife, Sophia, we might not have listed among the great names of literature the name of Nathaniel Hawthorne. When Nathaniel, a heartbroken man, went home to tell his wife that he was a failure and had been fired from his job in a customhouse, she surprised him with an exclamation of joy.

"Now," she said triumphantly, *"you can write your book!"*

"Yes," replied the man, with sagging confidence, *"and what shall we live on while I am writing it?"*

To his amazement, she opened a drawer and pulled out a substantial amount of money. *"Where on earth did you get that?"* he exclaimed.

"I have always known you were a man of genius," she told him. *"I knew that someday you would write a masterpiece. So every week, out of the money you gave me for housekeeping, I saved a little bit. So here is enough to last us for one whole year."* From her trust and confidence came

one of the greatest novels of American literature, **The Scarlet Letter.**

We need to be blessed. God is a God of blessing. Blessing pulls out the destiny that He has placed within us. Deep inside each of us is a divine purpose waiting to be set free. Books waiting to be written. Races waiting to be run. Plays waiting to be staged. Lives waiting to be lived. Risks waiting to be taken.

Beloved, we hold the keys. We have the power to speak curses or blessings into the lives of those we love. Could you unlock the destiny in someone's life today? All it takes is a word of encouragement... a smile... a hug.. a *"You can do it!"* Is there a book in you waiting to be written? A song waiting to be sung? A career waiting to be launched? A dream waiting to become reality? What are you waiting for? Go for it! So you make a mistake or two. Who hasn't? Babe Ruth led the majors in strike-outs the same year he hit sixty home runs. Thomas Edison failed over 10,000 times before he perfected the light bulb. Abraham Lincoln only won two elections in his life after many defeats, but one of his victories was the presidency of the United States.

When you come to the end of your life, you are going to be a *"has been,"* or a *"never was."* The choice is yours. Don't let the obstacles block the view of your destiny. Remember... bumps are what you climb on. Keep climbing, Beloved!

"Father, You are the God of all comfort and encouragement. We are never more like You than when we encourage one another. You know how much discouragement there is in this world. God forbid that I add to it. I fulfill my destiny whenever I help others to fulfill theirs. Thank You for believing in me enough to die for me. May I go and do likewise for You. Amen."

50

"Master," Simon replied, "we worked hard all last night and didn't catch a thing. But if you say so, we'll try again."
—Luke 5:5 NLT

∽

On Saturday night, January 8, 1983, I finally gave up... gave in... gave out... whatever you want to call it. The Lord had been dealing with me for several months about leaving the career I loved, coaching and teaching, and following Him to only He knew where. He confirmed His calling upon my life with His Word... Hebrews 11:8. ***"It was by faith that Abraham obeyed when God called him to leave home and go to another land that God would give him as his inheritance. He went without knowing where he was going."*** I still don't know where I'm going, but He's been faithful to hang in there with me.

My life verse for some years now has been Colossians 1:28. ***"Him we preach, warning every man and teaching every man in all wisdom, that we may present every man perfect in Christ Jesus"*** (NKJV). God put a burning desire in my heart to encourage people to be all they can be for Him. My motivational gift is encouragement with secondary gifts of service and mercy. I've been in the process of discipling and being discipled for 25 years now. There are times when I get tired of encouraging, studying, praying and witnessing.

Some people just don't want to change. Every once in a while, you just want to see some fruit for your labor. Know what I mean?

I've been feeling a little burned out for about a year now. God seems to be hiding from me. I don't feel His presence like I have at times in the past. Sometimes I feel like my prayers don't make it to the ceiling. I guess I'm tired of fishing and not catching anything.

Then I came across a Scripture I had read a hundred times, and it was like I had never seen it before. Has that ever happened to you? It seems that Jesus was attracting some pretty large crowds and so much so that He sought refuge in a boat on the shores of the Sea of Galilee. As He finished His discourse with the crowd, He told Simon Peter to launch his boat out into the deep water and let down his nets. There he would catch many fish.

I understand exactly how Simon felt. Peter was a fisherman. Jesus was a carpenter. What do carpenters know about fishing, right? But Jesus was more than a carpenter. Peter knew that you can't catch fish in the middle of the day. Fish surface to feed at night when the water is cooler. Peter was exhausted... burned out if you will... having fished all night in prime fishing time and catching absolutely nothing. But there was something about this mysterious carpenter/preacher...

"Master, we have toiled all night and caught nothing; nevertheless at Your word I will let down the net" (Luke 5:5 NKJV). Every sense... every feeling... everything in his being rebelled... *"This is a total waste of time and energy!"* But in spite of all his objections, there was that word... the "N" word... NEVERTHELESS! Jesus would later use it, too, when things didn't make sense to Him in the Garden of Gethsemane (Matthew 26:39). That one NEVERTHELESS provided salvation, forgiveness and peace for you and me and a boat load of fish for Peter.

I get tired, discouraged, depressed and burned out sometimes trying to follow the Lord and fulfill my destiny. I'm sure you do, too. But just as Peter said, *"Lord, at Thy Word, I will do what You say,"* the Lord has a Word for you and me. ***"He gives power to those who are tired and worn out; He offers strength to the weak. Even youths will become exhausted, and young men will give up. But those who wait on the LORD will find new strength. They will fly high on wings like eagles. They will run and not grow weary. They will walk and not faint"*** (Isaiah 40:29-31 NLT).

The operative word is ***wait***. In Hebrew, the word means *"to bind together, perhaps by twisting."* The picture I get from this definition is a tiny thread being twisted around a steel cable. The thread has no strength, but by twisting itself around the cable, the cable's strength becomes the thread's. Our strength is depleted most notably by the mundane routine of life. It's the walking that causes us to faint, not the great bursts of energy we produce in the grandiose earthshaking endeavors of life. It's the walking... the daily call to obedience to the divine mission He has so graciously called us to carry out. There's no spotlights or screaming fans to cheer us on. No cheerleaders or hype. It's just plain obedience. It's being loyal to our Master when no one is loyal to us. It's being faithful to the One called Faithful and True. That's where our destiny is fulfilled. That's where the victory is won. That's where He is glorified and our life is filled to overflowing with His love and peace... just like Peter's boat.

"Lord, when You filled Peter's boat with fish, he fell at Your feet and cried, 'Lord, depart from me for I am a sinful man!' I, too, am a sinful man. I'm selfish and self-centered. I want what I want when I want it. I seldom remember that You left heaven's glory where You were revered, honored, obeyed and worshiped to come to this cesspool of greed and hedonism to die in my place. You didn't have to do it,

but NEVERTHELESS You did. Thank goodness, You did. Forgive me. Give me another chance to cast my nets into the deep today. Amen."

51

Yes, I am the vine; you are the branches. Those who remain in Me, and I in them, will produce much fruit. For apart from Me you can do nothing. —John 15:5 NLT

Do we really believe that without Jesus we can do nothing? Do you acknowledge Jesus in ALL your ways (Proverbs 3:5-6)? Are you deathly afraid of making a decision apart from seeking the Lord's mind about the matter because you messed up so many times before when you didn't ask Him? Do you think it bothers Jesus to ask Him about what you consider trivial matters? Do you sometimes live like a "practical atheist"? Do you order and decide the course of your life without a second thought of God's opinion? Do you live at times as if the Lord did not exist? Think about it.

Do you see what I mean? We don't really think we are helpless and hopeless without Him, but we are indeed. As I meditated on this verse, the Lord gave me a visual impression. I saw the Lord watering flowers with a garden hose (a "hose pipe" in the South). He would adjust the water flow to suit His purposes. He would turn the nozzle for a fine mist to water the delicate pansies. Then He would re-adjust it for a forceful stream to wash the bark off the sidewalk. Again

He would twist the nozzle for a little more forceful, wide-arching spray to hose down the car prior to washing.

I asked the Lord, *"What are You trying to show me?"* This is what I heard him say, **"Kenny, you are the hose. The water represents My Life. I want to pour out My Life on whomever I choose. You are simply My vessel to carry Me where I want to go. I decide when to turn the water on and when to turn it off. I decide whether I will pour My Life out as a gentle mist, or as a fire hydrant. That's My call. I decide the amount, the direction and the flow. Your only responsibility is to stay in My hand. You don't clean, refresh, wash and renew. I do. You only provide the conduit through which I flow. If you get a kink in your life because of sin or disobedience and the flow of My Life is shut down, you become useless. To bring life to those dying in trespasses and sins is your purpose and mission in life. Will you let Me get the kinks out of your life so that I can flow through you as I choose?"**

"Lord, I am the hose. You are the Water. Don't let me get "kinky" on You! Lord, unclog me. Flow through me anyway You want today. Amen."

52

For rebellion is as the sin of witchcraft, and stubbornness is as iniquity and idolatry. — 1 Samuel 15:23 KJV

When the Israelites were coming out of Egypt, Amalek cowardly attacked them from the rear when they were tired and weary. There was no fear of God in Amalek, a descendant of Esau. God did not forget what the Amalekites did to His people. God told Moses that He would blot their remembrance from under heaven after the Israelites were settled into the promised land. God has a memory like an elephant. He never forgets... except our sins that are covered by the Blood of Christ.

In 1 Samuel 15, the prophet Samuel relayed God's message to King Saul. *"**This is what the LORD Almighty says:** '**I have decided to settle accounts with the nation of Amalek for opposing Israel when they came from Egypt. Now go and completely destroy the entire Amalekite nation--men, women, children, babies, cattle, sheep, camels, and donkeys'"***(vs. 3 NLT). Saul had his marching orders. However, instead of utterly destroying the Amalekites and every living thing they owned, Saul spared their king, Agag, and kept the best of the animals.

Then the word of the Lord came to His prophet, Samuel. **"I am sorry that I ever made Saul king, for he has not**

been loyal to Me and has again refused to obey Me" (1 Samuel 15:11 NLT). Samuel then went out to confront Saul. Upon his arrival, Saul greeted Samuel. *"May the Lord bless you. I have carried out the commandment of the Lord!"* Saul was proud of himself. He was fully convinced that he had done what the Lord wanted. He was deceived. Why? Because even the slightest disobedience gives ground to the deceiver. This was not the first time Saul had taken matters into his own hands.

When Saul first became the king, he called the troops together to engage the Philistines in battle. Samuel told Saul to wait seven days for him to come and offer sacrifices to the Lord and instruct Saul as the what the Lord would have him do. When Samuel did not show up, Saul became antsy and offered the sacrifices himself. A definite "no-no." Thus we see Saul's inherent lack of trust in the Lord at the very earliest stages of his reign. It was all the crack satan needed to sneak in and deceive Saul.

Because Saul failed to utterly destroy the Amalekites as the Lord had commanded, they came back to cause more trouble for the people of God. In 1 Samuel 30, we find the Amalekites, whom Saul should have destroyed, plundering Ziklag, the home base of David and his mighty men of valor. In addition to that, Haman, who plotted to eradicate the entire Jewish population during the reign of Queen Esther, was a descendant of Agag, the king Saul spared. As a result of his disobedience, the throne was torn from Saul's grasp, and he died a dishonorable death at the hands of his armor-bearer.

Beloved, listen to me. **Partial obedience is total rebellion to God.** Saul at one time had the Spirit of God upon his life. He was humble and submissive in the beginning. But because he feared people more than God, he failed to fulfill the destiny God had for him. His life was destroyed and many innocent people suffered because he failed to fully obey the Lord.

Precious saint, is there even the slightest area of disobedience in your life? The deceiver only needs a sliver of an opening to gain access to your life and utterly destroy you. Unlike Saul, satan will completely and totally devastate your life. Let's ask the Holy Spirit to search our hearts and reveal any disobedience and rebellion in our lives. Then let's confess, repent and ask Him to wash it away with the blood of Christ. Our lives and the lives of many we love hang in the balance, not to mention God's glory being stifled. Our enemy is ruthless and merciless. God is gracious and merciful. Watch and pray!

"God forbid that I dishonor You by my slightest disobedience to Your will. Father, if there is anything in my life displeasing to You, please reveal it to me. Forgive me. Have mercy upon me. I sit here and wait for You to search me with a fine-tooth comb. Cleanse me with the blood of Christ, and I will be clean. I wait upon You. Amen."

53

But I have this complaint against you. You don't love me or each other as you did at first! —Revelation 2:4 NLT

Remember when you first fell in love with your Sweetie? She was all you could think about. You walked around glassy-eyed with your head in the clouds all the time. The thought of her consumed every waking moment, and then you dreamed about her all night long. The mere anticipation of being with her set your heart racing and the butterflies churning. When you were together, you clung to her like a fly on a chocolate milkshake straw. Her every wish was your command. You couldn't do enough to please her. Remember?

Then you married her. You still loved her, but your heart rate dropped and the butterflies flew off somewhere. Your thoughts were captivated by climbing the career ladder and your dreams turned to nightmares about rat races and making ends meet. Her every wish became a nagging nuisance and being with her became commonplace. What in the world went wrong? You lost your first love. You let the tyranny of the urgent gain control of your priorities. In a word, you lost your zeal.

How do you get that 'lovin' feeling' back? I regret to say that it usually takes a major wake-up call. Several years ago, we moved to Shelby to win the world for Jesus. I was consumed with ministry, not Christ, but ministry. I was bound and determined to do something for Jesus. After all, He had done so much for me, I needed to pay Him back (like I could do that). Wanda got put on the back burner. I was consumed with church and meeting the felt needs of an ever increasing flock of unruly sheep.

Then God intervened... mercifully and graciously. Wanda was diagnosed with breast cancer. All of a sudden, my world crumbled before my very eyes. I was in danger of losing the most important thing God had given me on this earth... my Bride. Talk about a wake-up call! The little petty problems that I considered earth-shattering dwindled to nothing. The church, the ministry, my calling... all seemed so meaningless and unimportant compared to losing my wife and the mother of my children. God re-ordered my priorities in a heartbeat!

Wanda spent a year of agony recovering from the mastectomy and reconstruction surgery. I spent a year thanking God for sparing my life and showing me what's really important. I begged Him and still do beg Him not to let me take things for granted anymore. That's how we lose our first love. We start taking Him and His blessings for granted. The first thing to go is our attitude of gratitude. Familiarity breeds contempt. We begin to think God owes us the air we breathe, our spouses, our families, our health, warm showers, sweet tea, crock pot pintos and onions, sunshine, golf courses, and all the finer things in life. We cannot say "thank you" enough, especially to God. In Him we live and move and have our being (Acts 17:28). He holds all things together from atoms to marriages (Colossians 1:17). He gives us everything we need to live a full, abundant and godly life (2 Peter 1:3). If God pulled the plug, we would be down the tubes. He is God. We are not. Sometimes it takes a catastrophe to make us realize that.

Beloved, have you lost your love for God? Do you love Him today like you did when He first saved you? What happened? Did you lose your "attitude of gratitude"? Did you start taking Him and all His provisions and blessings for granted? Are you ready to get your priorities in order? Then let's do it!

"Father God, I have lost my zeal and love for You. You have been so faithful in spite of my unfaithfulness. I'm so sorry that I have taken You for granted. Please forgive me. Would You help me to restore my "attitude of gratitude"? Grant me the discipline and the courage to say 'no' to the tyrant of urgency... those things that cry out DO ME NOW! Lord, I want You to be the number one priority in my life. I am all Yours. I am nothing without You. Bring me to the full awareness of that fact. My sole desire is to glorify You and enjoy You forever. Today is the first day of the rest of my life... Your Life. I am living on borrowed time since You saved me. Help Yourself to me today, Lord. I serve at the pleasure of the King. It would be nice to have the butterflies back, Father! I love You, and I praise you in the matchless Name of Your Son and my Savior, the Lord Jesus Christ. Amen."

54

"If you had one hundred sheep, and one of them strayed away and was lost in the wilderness, wouldn't you leave the ninety-nine others to go and search for the lost one until you found it?" —Luke 15:4 NLT

You all remember Yoda, the little stray 4-week old kitten we picked up on the side of the road a few weeks ago. When we picked her up, she was blind in one eye, inundated with flees and mere hours away from going home to be with Jesus. We literally snatched her from the jaws of death. You should see her now after being in Wanda's intensive care unit for four weeks. She bounces around the house getting into everything. Now I know why they say, "curiosity killed the cat."

Wanda loves that cat which she affectionately calls, Yoda Pooh. She snuggles that cat in her arms like a baby and talks baby-talk while gently patting her to sleep. The polls are tipping in Yoda's favor as to whom will get to stay in the house... me or her. If the vote came today, it would be a tight race. I shudder to think about it.

Although she is a nuisance and an allergy time bomb, Yoda is growing on me. She is a sight to watch. She will bow up and hop sideways as she stalks Snuggles who pays her about as much attention as a rhinoceros does a fly. She will attack my legs while I watch television and get up in my plate while I'm trying to eat my supper. She is kinda cute... for a cat.

Last night, God used that little fur ball to demonstrate His magnificent love and compassion. Wanda went to bed around 11 pm. I stayed up to watch ESPN to catch up on the college football scores for the day. About 11:30, I let Snuggles out. When Snuggles came back inside, I called Yoda to put her up for the night. She was nowhere to be found. We turned the house upside down looking for her. I knew she had been in the study because there was a potted plant turned over. Still, we called and called... *"Yoda! Where are you?"* but she had vanished into thin air.

Wanda and I walked the neighborhood with a flashlight looking for the little booger. I thought we were going to get shot walking through our neighbors' yards at midnight shining a flashlight in their flower beds whisperingly shouting, *"Yoda! Yoda! Come here girl!"* You know cats are not like dogs. Dogs will lay their ears back, hang their tongue out the side of their mouth and run to you whenever you call them. Cats just sit there and look at you like you're crazy.

Having searched the adjacent yards, we drove around the block in the car shining the flashlight at people's houses. I kept waiting for the police to come up and arrest us for disturbing the peace. About 1 o'clock, we gave up the search and went to bed. I told Wanda that we needed to pray for Yoda. I prayed, *"Lord, you know where Yoda is right now. You can see her right where she is. Would you protect her and take care of her tonight. If you send someone to find her, let them take good care of her. If it's Your will, bring her back home to us. Thanks. Amen."* And we went to sleep.

The next morning while I was dressing for church, I heard Snuggles "grark"...that's a half grunt and a half bark. It's what she does when Yoda bows up and lunges at her to get her to play. I ran into the den and there lay Snuggles with Yoda bouncing around like a flea on a hot plate. Yoda had crawled up inside the entertainment center in the study after she had knocked the plant over. She was afraid and hid to avoid the punishment. She stayed there all night. She reminded me of how we all deal with our faults and sin. We run away from the only One Who really loves and cares for us... the only One Whose arms remain open whenever we fall inviting us to come home and be forgiven and restored. How crazy we are to run away and hide. How much pain we must cause Him to endure.

As I reflect back on that fateful night when we thought we had lost Yoda, I couldn't help but think of how the Lord came to seek and to save that which was lost (Luke 19:10). The Lord does, indeed, leave the 99 sheep and seek the one who strays and loses his way. There we were walking around the neighborhood in our pajamas looking for a worthless little furball and crying ourselves to sleep over her when she provides no lasting benefit for our family. She does no work. She just eats and gets into everything and has to be monitored every minute to keep her from killing herself. But we love her. I guess we love her because she is so much like us. We, too, were abused and abandoned by the enemy of our souls, tormented by the flesh, the world and the devil and left on the side of the road to die. We have to be constantly monitored by the Lord to keep us from killing ourselves. Then Someone stopped and picked us up. We had nothing to offer Him but brokenness and strife, yet He took us in anyway, doctored us up and loved us to life... kinda like we did for Yoda. I guess that's why she's become so special. She reminds me of the Father's never-ending, ever-pursuing love and grace.

If I ever had a question about how much He loves you and me, He provided the answer one Saturday night in the form of a tiny furball named, Yoda, who lost her way... accidently on purpose.

"Heavenly Father, thank You for pursuing a love relationship with me that is real and personal. You did more than search my neighborhood for me in the middle of the night. You sent Your Son and My Lord to die in my place. Your love is too much for me to comprehend. I cannot fathom it all. Even though I can't understand, I do enjoy it. I love You, too, Father. Thanks for stopping to pick me up and taking such good care of me. Amen."

55

For You created everything, and it is for Your pleasure that they exist and were created. —Revelation 4:11 NLT

Eric Liddel was a Scottish track star who ran in the 1924 Olympics in Paris. The hope of a gold medal for his beloved Scotland rested upon the wings of his feet. But as much as he loved his country, he loved the Lord even more. As great a runner as he was, he is most famous for his boycott of the Olympic games. When Eric was scheduled to run one of his races on a Sunday, he refused to do so. His convictions were more precious to him than gold. How many saints are left like that today?

Eric made a statement that has intrigued me for years. He said, *"God made me to run fast. I feel His pleasure when I run."* God made us for His pleasure. He created us exactly like He wanted. Height. Weight. Hair color. No hair. Short. Tall. Talents. Abilities. Gifts. Everything. We are just what Father wants us to be. We were created for His pleasure. Life becomes "un-pleasurable" when we try to be something we weren't created to be. Fish hate to run but love to swim. Get the picture?

Whenever we live and perform in the way He created us, He is ecstatically delighted, and we feel His pleasure, too. The reason we do not feel His pleasure is because we let the world, the flesh and the devil talk us into pleasing ourselves and others rather than God. The world's chief goal is to turn us into malcontents. Ever notice how advertisers try to convince us that what we don't exactly have what we need? There once was a cigarette commercial that used to claim that it was "the one that satisfies." Well, if it satisfies, why couldn't you smoke one and never need another?

A youth minister once asked his youth group this question: *"If you had the power to change anything about your appearance, would you use it?"* Ninety-five percent said that they would. For whose pleasure do most people think they were created? Who are we trying to please? A fickle world which is never satisfied? People who have no idea what they really want? We try to please everyone but God. Why? We falsely believe that things and people can meet the deep needs of our heart. They never could and never will be able to do that. We were not created for things or people. We were created by and for a loving Heavenly Father Who made us just the way He wanted. He made us for His pleasure. The pleasure we are seeking is found only in being who He created us to be.

What are you good at? What thrills your heart? I'm in my element when I encourage people. I feel His pleasure whenever He begins to flow through me whenever I'm teaching or writing. I love music and could have been a decent pianist, but I let people tell me that only sissies play the piano. That is one pleasure I stifled for both of us. Beloved, don't let that happen to you. Don't let the world dictate to you who you should be. Father God is the only One Who has that right. Be all you can be for Him.

The next time you feel the pleasure and joy of a job well done, remember that you are tickling the heart of God as well. Enjoy!

"Heavenly Father, thank You for creating me for Your pleasure. Forgive me for trying to live my way rather than Yours. I cannot do everything. You didn't intend for me to do everything. But some things I do very, very well. Thank You for reminding me that it is Your pleasure that I feel when I do those things. Thanks for sharing Your pleasure with me. Be pleased in me today, Lord. Amen."

56

All the peoples of the earth are regarded as nothing. He does as He pleases with the powers of heaven and the peoples of the earth. No one can hold back His hand or say to Him: "What have You done?" —Daniel 4:35 NIV

Has it ever occurred to you that nothing has ever occurred to God? Nothing ever catches God by surprise. He is in absolute control over all of His creation. He does whatever pleases Him anytime, anyway, anyhow. Knowing that God is sovereign in His rule is quite comforting if what pleases God is pleasing to us. When our biopsies come back benign, or we get a promotion, or our marriages are sweeter than wine, we delight in the fact that God is pleasing us by what pleases Him. But how do we respond to His sovereignty when the biopsy comes back malignant, or we lose our jobs, or our covenant partner leaves home for someone else? At times like these, it can be very difficult to trust God.

God's sovereignty can be really scary if we don't understand the total nature of God. There are three essential truths we must believe (cling to, trust in, rely upon, put your whole weight upon) if we are going to trust God when the bottom falls out. First of all, God is completely sovereign. He is also perfect in His love. And finally, He is infinite in His wisdom.

God is love. We cannot fathom the depths of His love for us as His children. He loved us so much that while we were still sinners, He sent His Son, Jesus, to die for us. He gave us the best. Do you think He's going to keep the rest? I don't think so. *"If God is for us, who can ever be against us? Since God did not spare even His own Son but gave Him up for us all, won't God, Who gave us Christ, also give us everything else?"* (Romans 8:31-32 NLT). God can never act in any way toward us that is not in accord with His character, and God is perfect love.

God is infinitely wise. He sees the beginning and the end while we are barely able to see the middle. **"Only I can tell you what is going to happen even before it happens. Everything I plan will come to pass, for I do whatever I wish"** (Isaiah 46:10-11 NLT). The Lord is too smart to ever make a mistake. He never miscalculates. He never says, "Ooops!" He knows some stuff. He knows what's best for me... and for you. **"For I know the plans I have for you,"** *says the LORD.* **"They are plans for good and not for disaster, to give you a future and a hope"** (Jeremiah 29:11 NLT). God is orchestrating everything in our lives so that we can fulfill the wonderful destiny He's planned for us. *"You chart the path ahead of me and tell me where to stop and rest. Every moment You know where I am. You saw me before I was born. Every day of my life was recorded in Your book. Every moment was laid out before a single day had passed"* (Psalm 139:6 & 16 NLT). Having penned this marvelous truth, the psalmist exclaimed, *"Such knowledge is too wonderful for me!"* Me, too!

Even if God is perfect in His love and infinitely wise, it won't do us any good if God does not have the power to pull off His plans. But rest assured, Beloved, He is absolute in His power as well. *"Ah, Sovereign LORD, You have made the heavens and the earth by Your great power and outstretched arm. Nothing is too hard for You"* (Jeremiah

32:17 NIV). *"I know that You can do all things; no plan of Yours can be thwarted"* (Job 42:2 NIV).

Mighty soldier of the Lord, God loves you far too much to do anything that would ultimately hurt or harm you. He does all things for your good and for His glory. He is too wise to ever make a mistake. He knows what's best even though oftentimes it doesn't appear that way in this temporal life. And above all, He has the power to bring it all about. Nothing is too difficult for God. Cancer? Broken relationships? Depression? Miscarriage? Finances? Rebellious kids? Sin? NOTHING! ABSOLUTELY NOTHING is beyond the scope of God's love, wisdom and sovereign power. He is great and greatly to be praised!

When are you going to stop fretting and start resting in Him? He's got everything under His control. He is waiting for you to give up yours.

"Heavenly Father, sometimes I feel like a man lying tensely in a bed waiting for it to collapse. My tenseness will not keep it from falling and will only make the jolt worse when and if it does fall. I am worn out from worrying about things that are beyond my control. I'm finding that control is just an illusion. I don't have control over anything, but You do. Lord, I'm surrendering to You today. I'm giving up control. I'm going to trust You today no matter what. I agree with the Apostle Paul who said, 'I know the One in Whom I trust, and I am sure that He is able to guard what I have entrusted to Him until the day of His return' (2 Tim 1:12 NLT). Be it unto me according to Your Word. Amen."

57

And the Holy Spirit helps us in our distress. For we don't even know what we should pray for, nor how we should pray. But the Holy Spirit prays for us with groanings that cannot be expressed in words. —Romans 8:26 NLT

Do you remember the story in Mark chapter 2 when the four men lowered their paralytic friend down through a hole in the roof in order to get him to Jesus? The men brought their friend to Jesus for physical healing, but note the first thing Jesus said to him. ***Seeing their faith, Jesus said to the paralyzed man,* "My son, your sins are forgiven"** (Mark 2:5). He didn't ask for forgiveness. He didn't even ask for healing. His friends just dropped Him down in front of Jesus. But Jesus knew what he really needed. He knows what we all need.

How many times do we tell Jesus what we *think* we need? "Lord, I need my wife fixed." *Lord, if you can come through for me this time, I'll serve You forever."* "Lord, I need a job." And on and on... But Jesus knows what we really need. We need Him. We need to be totally dependent on Him. We need to totally trust in Him. We need to really believe that without Him we can do nothing (John 15:5). We need to thank Him when the bottom falls out because the bottom is what keeps us from falling into His lap. That's what we really need.

I have a poem in my office that illustrates the fact that we don't know how to pray. Allow me to share it with you.

> *I asked God for strength that I may achieve.*
> *I was made weak so that I could learn to humbly obey.*
> *I asked God for health that I may do great things. I was given infirmity that I may do better things.*
> *I asked God for riches that I might be happy. I was given poverty that I may be wise.*
> *I asked God for power that I might have the praise of men. I was given weakness that I may feel the need of God.*
> *I asked God for all things that I might enjoy life. I was given life that I may enjoy all things.*
> *I got nothing I asked for, but everything I had hoped for.*
> *Almost despite myself, my unspoken prayers were answered.*
> *I am among all most richly blessed.*

"Heavenly Father, thank You for answering my unspoken prayers. Thank You for knowing what I really need. Lord, in the future, if I ever ask You for something, and You have something better for me, then please cancel my first request. Amen."

58

For the Lord your God has arrived to live among you. He is a mighty Savior. He will give you victory. He will rejoice over you with great gladness; He will love you and not accuse you. Is that a joyous choir I hear? No, it is the Lord Himself exulting over you in happy song.
—Zephaniah 3:17 TLB

Life can be pretty discouraging at times. It will knock you down and grind your nose in the dirt. It can be merciless and heartless. Is there anyone out there who really cares about what we're going through? According to our verse today, there is.

The Lord gets a lot of bad press because we tend to project onto Him the attitude and actions of people. For instance, some people will promise to do something for you and then never show up. Some of those people are the ones you love, trust and have high expectations for... family, teachers, ministers, etc.. Most of us have been disappointed with those who should love and care for us the most. Whenever we expect God to act the same way that people act toward us, we get a distorted picture of Who He really is and how He really feels. Then we become disappointed with God because we think He doesn't love or care for us either.

Someone once told me that in order to enjoy, not just endure life, we need five people whose faces light up every time they see us. We all need people who love us just the way we are... warts and all. People who just plain enjoy being around us. They want nothing from us but our company. They just like us. Problem is that most of us don't have one person like that, much less five. Human nature by nature is selfish and soulish. We tend to have hidden agendas in our relationships. We tend to love people on the condition that they do or be something for our benefit. When we don't get what we want out of a relationship, our human nature will discard it like an orange peel with all the juice sucked out. The world is strewn with dried up orange peels.

The reason most people walk around like they've been weaned on dill pickles is because their belief system has accepted a lie as the truth. They believe that God loves the way people love. Thank goodness that is not true. But if you believe that lie, then the lie becomes truth for you. *"For as a man thinks in his heart, so is he"* (Proverbs 23:7).

I have a difficult time believing that God rejoices over me... that His face lights up every time He thinks about me... that He sings a happy song over me. I know me. I'm selfish, mean, hateful... let's stop there. If I act like that around people, I know how they will treat me... orange peel city. It's just plain hard for me to believe that anyone could love and enjoy being around such a self-centered human being as me, much less God. But that's what the Word of God says. He loves me unconditionally regardless of my attitude and actions. Yeah, He hates my sin, but He loves me. I know that in my head, but my heart is still waiting to be informed. Know what I mean?

Why don't we pray and ask God to lower the Truth about eighteen inches from our heads to our hearts. I'm tired of dried-up orange peels, aren't you?

"Dear Lord, I'm so sorry that I expect people to be perfect like You. I'm even sorrier that I turn around and expect You to act like people. But my life experiences have so ingrained this 'orange peel' mentality that I can't seem to get over it. Lord, would You come and cleanse me of my 'stinking thinking.' Would You make the truth of Your unconditional love for me real? I know You can and are most willing to do it. And Lord, would You come and live Your life through me today? Would You let the light of Your face shine through mine so that I can be one of those faces that light up for other orange peel people? I can't think of anything else that would light up my face any quicker than knowing that You love me enough to live and shine through me. Shine, Jesus, shine! Amen."

59

There is really only one thing worth being concerned about. Mary has discovered it--and I won't take it away from her.
—Luke 10:42 NLT

The flesh can't rest. It has to be doing something. It hungers for approval... a way of measuring its worth and value. That is why the flesh loves the Law of God. It becomes frustrated that it cannot attain to the Law's perfection, but the Law makes a great measuring device for comparison to others. *"I read my Bible... I pray... I go to church... I do good deeds... I don't drink, cuss, smoke, or chew, or go with girls who do. I am good. Look what I do compared to you!"*

The flesh never understands that we are not who we are because of what we do. We do what we do because of Whose we are. Jesus has already done for us everything that ever needed doing. Because of His doing, we can simply rest in Him and allow Him to live in and through us. We don't stop doing, but our doing is in the power of the Spirit and not of the flesh.

God's people have always struggled with fleshly doing. **"God will speak to this people, 'This is the resting place, let the weary rest'; and, 'This is the place of repose'--but they would not listen. So then, the Word of the LORD to them will become: Do and do, do and do, rule on rule, rule** *on rule; a little here, a little there-- so that they will go and fall backward, be injured and snared and captured"* (Isa 28:11-13 NIV). Whenever we try to earn approval and acceptance via our performance, frustration and disappointment hound us every step of the way. Until we give up trying, we do and do to the point of exhaustion. Then we re-dedicate our lives to God and vow to do better next time. And then the cycle starts all over again. Some just give up and quit trying. Others are too stubborn to quit. Few discover the reality of entering into His rest.

In Luke chapter 10, we find Jesus paying a visit to the home of Martha and Mary, Lazarus' sisters. Martha is in the kitchen working herself into a dither trying to prepare a great meal for the Lord. Mary is in the living room sitting at His feet soaking in His presence. Martha is ticked off. *"Lord, tell Mary to get off her blessed assurance and get in here to help me. Who does she think she is?"* Jesus' answer goes right to the source of Martha's frustration. **"My dear Martha, you are so upset over all these details! There is really only one thing worth being concerned about. Mary has discovered it--and I won't take it away from her"** (Luke 10:41-42 NLT).

Did you notice how Jesus addressed Martha? **"Dear Martha..."** You can almost feel His love and acceptance of her even though she is 180 degrees off course. He still loves her and longs for her to end her frustration by simply doing the only thing that really matters... trusting and resting in Him and His love. Mary found that ONE thing and the Lord commended her. And she wasn't doing a thing.

Years ago when I really became serious about serving the Lord, I would constantly ask God what I could do for Him. If I was not doing something of eternal value like reading the Bible, or praying, or witnessing, I felt like the Lord was disappointed in me. The only time I ever felt any value was when I was doing something for the Lord. Then one day, the

Lord answered me. **"So, Kenny, you want to do something for Me. Okay, here is what I want you to do. Sit down and let's talk. I want to hang out with you, but you are so busy running around doing something FOR Me that you never have time to be WITH Me. Stay here with Me until leaving My presence to do something for Me is the last thing you want to do. Then you will be ready to do something."**

I'll have to admit that for a while, I felt like I was backslidden. I realized that I had become a "human doing," not a "human being." All the things I did because I thought the Lord wanted me to do them, I cut them out. The Lord began to pull off my grave clothes of legalism, perfectionism and fleshly doing. He's still working on me. I still feel the flesh raise up its ugly old head every now and then, but now I stop and rest in Him.

Looks like you could use a rest yourself. If you just have to DO something, run on over and jump in His lap. That's all you need to DO!

"Heavenly Father, the joy of the Lord is my strength. Sometimes I feel like all my strength is gone. Doing and doing and doing has taken its toll on me and robbed me of Your joy. I need Your grace now not to do something, but to stop doing those things that You never asked me to do. Is it okay if I just rest here with You awhile? Thanks, Lord, for all You've done! Amen."

60

*My prayer for all of them is that they will be one,
just as You and I are one, Father--that just as You are in Me
and I am in You, so they will be in us, and the world
will believe You sent me.* —John 17:21 NLT

This is Jesus' prayer, and Jesus always gets His prayers answered. Why? Because He is one with His Father. He only prays for what His Father desires. Whatever Father God wants, Jesus prays for. And when Jesus prays for it, Father God gives what Jesus asks for.

Now, let's get to the point. We are made and created for God, not for ourselves. Not for service, but for God Himself. He loves us more than we will ever be able to comprehend. How could Father give His Son to die such a cruel death for you and me? I know me. I'm mean, self-absorbed, self-centered, etc. Nothing good dwells in me but Jesus. I am rotten to the core. I don't know about you, but my guess is that you are, too. In spite of that, **"God made Him (Jesus) Who had no sin to be sin for us, so that in Him we might become the righteousness of God"** (2 Corinthians 5:21 NIV).

There is a verse of Scripture that I used to take great delight in until the Lord showed me what it really meant. **"As He is, so are we in this world"** (1 John 4:17 KJV). I thought this verse meant that I would be kind, loving, gentle, compassionate and miracle-working filled will knowledge and revelation just like Jesus. Then the Lord showed me some other Scriptures that I had not taken into consideration. ***"Then He went down with them and came to Nazareth, and was subject to them"*** (Luke 2:51 NKJV). Jesus was ready at twelve years old to begin His ministry, but His Mom and Dad didn't understand. So He submitted to their authority. He didn't demand His own way. He lived at home for thirty years with brothers and sisters who didn't believe in Him. And when He began His ministry after that, they said He was crazy.

Jesus was despised and rejected, misrepresented and misunderstood. As He is, so are we in this world. We become disillusioned if we think we are built for ourselves and not for God. The servant is not better than his Master. If they treated our Master this way, what makes you think the world will treat us any different. God allows the devil, sin and bad people to triumph at times. These things either make us bitter or better... villains or saints... friends or foes of God. It depends entirely on our relationship with God. We are either becoming more like our Father in heaven, or we are becoming more self-absorbed.

God does not exist to answer our prayers, but our prayers are lifted so that we can know the mind of God... what He desires. What does God desire? He desires what Jesus prayed for... **"that we may be one, just as God the Father, God the Son and God the Holy Spirit are One."** God has one prayer He must answer, and that is the prayer of Jesus. I don't care how imperfect and immature you are as a disciple of Christ, when you pray Jesus' prayer, God will answer if you hang in there and not give up.

The Apostle Paul, himself, said that he didn't know why he did what he did at times. God will not leave us alone until we are one with Him. Jesus asked Father to do that, and Father is going to grant His request regardless of what it takes. If you didn't know it before, you should now... there is a risk in discipleship. God never shields us from the world, the flesh and the devil. God is not into "show business." He is into building character... the character of His Son into each of us. When satan sought to sift Peter like wheat (King James for "turn him every which way but loose"), Jesus told Peter that He had prayed that his faith would not fail (Luke 22:31-32). Notice that Jesus did not pray that satan wouldn't do it, but that when he did, Peter's faith would be strong and unfailing.

Beloved, are you frustrated and despairing over the fact that no one understands you and all you are going through? Nobody understands. We are a mystery even to ourselves. Nobody understands you like Jesus. Hand yourself over to Him. If we understand what God is after, we will be saved from being mean and self-absorbed. In the end, that's all we really need to understand.

"Lord, make me one... heart, mind and soul... with You and Father God. Amen."

61

A man with leprosy came to Him and begged Him on his knees, "If You are willing, You can make me clean."
—Mark 1:40 NIV

I've been on a quest to become a pray-er. I want to learn how to pray fervently and effectually. The Lord has really been impressing upon me about the absolute necessity of prayer. It's almost as if He is begging us to pray. He implores us to ask and promises that what we ask will be given to us... if we seek, we shall find... if we knock, it will be opened (Luke 11:9). He assures us that if we ask anything according to His will, He will do it (I John 5:14-15). He reproves us saying that we don't have because we don't ask (James 4:2). He promises that whatever we ask Him, believing, we will receive (Matthew 21:22).

In light of these magnificent promises, why are we not charging hell with a water pistol? Why are we such miserable people? Go to Wal-Mart and watch people. Look into their dead eyes. For most, there is no light. No joy. No evident eternal purpose or meaning to their lives. Why is that so when we have such a marvelous Savior Who would fill their deepest need in a heartbeat if they would only come to Him?

I think it has a lot to do with how we approach the Lord. For instance, take the leper in Mark 1:40-45. Notice first of all how he came to Jesus. He came begging on his knees in utter humility giving the Lord the honor and reverence due His Name. He knew the hopelessness of his situation apart from Christ and came totally dependent upon Him to meet His need. Until we realize how helpless we are, there is no hope for our predicament.

Secondly, the leper had absolute trust in the power of Christ to heal him. *"You can make me clean."* Note that he did not say, *"You have the power to heal people."* He said, *"You can make ME clean."* Many people wrongly believe that the Lord forgives, heals and blesses other people, but not themselves personally. If you are to receive His will for your life, you must truly believe that He not only wants to, but has the power to do it for YOU. He loves YOU as much as He loves anyone else. You must believe which means "cling to, trust in, rely upon, put your whole weight upon" the object of your belief.

Next, the leper submitted to the Lord's will. *"If You are willing, You can make me clean."* I'm sure the leper, like most of us, had no doubt of Christ's willingness to give general help to those in distress, but he modestly came to Jesus desiring only that His will be done, not his own. This humble appeal from a lowly outcast moved the heart of the King of kings with compassion. The leper's unassuming faith, humility and submission blessed our Lord. As you read the passage, you can almost hear the heartcry of Jesus... **"Am I willing? Are you kidding? Of course, I am willing!"**

What Jesus did next must have been incomprehensible. Jesus reached out His hand and touched the leper. In that culture, a leper was untouchable. He even had to walk far away from people and warn them as they approached with a loud shout, *"Unclean! Unclean!"* Can you even begin to imagine a life like that? The humiliation... the loneliness...

the emotional, not to mention the physical suffering... To have anyone willingly touch you would have been a blessing of gigantic proportion, but for the Lord of glory Himself to touch you...

I truly believe that had the Lord's will for him been to remain a leper, His touch would have been more than sufficient. But our Lord's desire is to fill our cups to overflowing with His goodness and mercy. ***"Immediately the leprosy left him and he was cured."*** Whenever God finds faith coupled with humility and obedience, He immediately dispenses His will. Oh, that we were as quick to trust as He is to perform.

"Dear Lord, why am I so hard-headed? Why would I think You can and will do for others but not for me? False humility is the worst form of pride. You hate pride, Lord. Please forgive me. If You are willing, You can fix me. Be it unto me, according to Your Word. Amen."

62

And you husbands must love your wives with the same love Christ showed the church. He gave up His life for her...
—Ephesians 5:25 NLT

A love affair of some 62 years, 8 months and 11 days ended Sunday morning, September 14, 2003 at 4:30 a.m.. My Mom went home to be with the Lord. Pop and Nanna met in an ice cream shop in the summer of 1939. At the memorial service, Pop said she was the prettiest thing he ever saw the first time he met her, and she was the prettiest thing he ever saw the day she died.

I've heard it said that values are *caught*, not *taught*. Nanna and Pop never went to seminars on marriage and parenting. They never quoted Scripture to me and my sister. They just lived out Micah 6:8. They did what was right, they loved mercy and accepted everyone just as they were, and they always walked in humility before the Lord. They were great role models.

They say the best thing a father can do for his children is to love their mother. Well, Pop aced that one. Nanna had many health problems with close to forty hospital stays during their 62 years together. Pop nursed her... cared for her... pampered her 24/7. The last year of her life, Pop woke up every two hours during the night to check on her. He slept on the couch right next to her bed for better than a year.

I've watched Pop feed her supplement with a syringe because she was unable to chew her food. He would feed her a little bit and then wipe her mouth and say, *"Is that good, Honey? Let me get that off your mouth."* Then he would bend down and kiss her and say, *"I love you."* Nanna would muster up enough strength to say, *"I love you, too."* You could go to a thousand marriage seminars and not learn what I've learned about what it takes to make a marriage blissful just by watching them.

When Nanna and Pop married, Pop had fifteen dollars and no place to live. All they had was each other and a pot full of hopes and aspirations. They struggled just like all couples struggle... bills, business, illness, separation during WWII, raising kids and all the other nagging little things that seek to steal joy and contentment. The same sun that grows the crops also bakes the soil and makes it hard. The hard times they experienced simply tempered their resolve and faith in the Lord and caused their love to flourish and grow. Adversity either makes us *bitter* or *better*. The choice is ours to make. Nanna and Pop chose wisely.

I am so blessed to have been raised in a home full of love. Everyone loves Nanna and Pop. Anyone and everyone who came to our home was hugged and kissed before they left. I mean... everyone. It didn't matter if you were a prince or a pauper. Everyone was loved and respected and made to feel like part of the family. That's why people loved to come to Nanna and Pop's house. It was a place that made you feel like you belonged... kinda like heaven is going to be.

They are the kind of people that make you feel your best whenever you are around them. I think Jesus was like that. Pop didn't learn that from a Bible study. He learned how to love from the Master Lover, Himself. Pop is the closest thing I've ever seen on this earth to Jesus. I don't say that because

Pop is so special, even though he is. I say that because Pop is a man who's word is his word. He is a man of honesty and integrity who means what he says and says what he means. When he gave his heart to the Lord, he held nothing back. In return, Jesus has lived His life full and free through Pop.

I was reminded this week of the really important things in life... my faith, my family and my friends. No amount of money, position or power can obtain the heritage that I have inherited from Nanna and Pop. Loving God and loving people is all that really matters. I think God agrees.

I close with a little bit of advice: Never leave the people you love without telling them you love them. Hug your spouse and children often. Kiss them more. Enjoy them more. Savor your friendships. Love people just the way they are. Let God change them if need be. Just love them. Enjoy life. Light candles instead of cursing the darkness. Be thankful for what you have and quit grumbling about what you don't have. Smile more. Frown less. Look for opportunities to pat others on the back and encourage them. Pull out the very best in others. Help others fulfill their destiny, and you will find your own fulfilled. Today is the first day of the rest of your life. When your attitude is right, there are no endings... only beginnings.

There's no time like the present to make Jesus *your* Final Answer! Pop and Nanna had no unanswered questions. He'll answer yours as well.

"Heavenly Father, what a good Daddy you are. Thanks for the blessing of a godly home. For those reading this today who were not blessed with such a home, give them grace to start one of their own. Grant them a new beginning... a new godly heritage to pass along to their children and their children's children. May we fill the world with Your love and grace one person... one family at a time. I love You today. Amen."

63

Therefore, anyone who becomes as humble as this little child is the greatest in the Kingdom of Heaven.
—Matthew 18:4 NLT

I want to be great in the Kingdom of Heaven, don't you? Therefore, I am hereby officially tendering my resignation as an adult. I have decided I would like to accept the responsibilities of an 8 year-old again. I want to go to McDonald's and think that it's a four-star restaurant. I want to sail sticks across a fresh mud puddle and make a sidewalk with rocks. I want to think M&M's are better than money because you can eat them. I want to lie under a big oak tree and run a lemonade stand with my friends on a hot summer's day. I want to return to a time when life was simple. When all you knew were colors, multiplication tables, and nursery rhymes, but that didn't bother you, because you didn't know what you didn't know, and you didn't care. All you knew was to be happy because you were blissfully unaware of all the things that should make you worried or upset.

I want to think the world is fair. That everyone is honest and good. I want to believe that anything is possible. I want to be oblivious to the complexities of life and be overly excited by the little things. I want to live simple again. I don't want my day to consist of computer crashes, mountains of paper-

Jesus... My Final Answer

work, depressing news, how to survive more days in the month than there is money in the bank, doctor bills, gossip, illness and loss of loved ones. I want to believe in the power of smiles, hugs, a kind word, truth, justice, peace, dreams, the imagination, mankind, and making angels in the snow. So... here's my checkbook and my car-keys, my credit card bills and my 401K statements. I am officially resigning from adulthood. And if you want to discuss this further, you'll have to catch me first, 'cause... *"Tag! You're it."*

"Heavenly Father, I believe that 'busy' means 'being under satan's yoke.' I'm too busy. Oh, yeah, I'm busy doing good things... reading the Bible, praying, witnessing, studying, working, going to meetings, saving the world for Jesus, but I'm missing You. I'm missing just being with You... hanging out with You... and running by all the best blessings in life... talking to grandkids on the phone... taking a boy fishing... walking in the rain... belly laughing... You know... the good stuff. I know you won't let me resign from adulthood, but you do want to remind me that I'll always be a child in Your eyes. And that's okay. It's better than okay. It's mandatory. Today, I want to play... but not hide-and-seek. I'm tired of hiding. I'm coming out to play. Amen."

64

*I assure you, until heaven and earth disappear,
even the smallest detail of God's law will remain until its
purpose is achieved.* —Matthew 5:18 NLT

Some people are so closed-minded that there's a vacuum in their skulls. Others are so open-minded that their brains are falling out. When it comes to God's Word, we must always remain open and teachable. However, once we embrace the Truth, there is no room for compromise, or broad-mindedness. God's spiritual laws are more binding and significant than natural laws. For example...

> There is no room for broad-mindedness in the chemical laboratory. Water is composed of two parts hydrogen and one part oxygen. The slightest deviation from that formula is forbidden.
>
> There is no room for broad-mindedness in music. The skilled director will not permit his first violin to deviate even so much as a note off the written measure, chord or key.
>
> There is no room for broad-mindedness in the mathematics classroom. Neither geometry, calculus nor

trigonometry allows any variation from exact accuracy, even for old time's sake. The solution of the problem is either right or it is wrong... no tolerance whatsoever.

There is no room for broad-mindedness in biology. One varying result out of a thousand experiments will invalidate an entire theory.

There is no room for broad-mindedness on the athletic field. The game is to be played according to the rules with no favors shown for "charity's sake."

There is no room for broad-mindedness in the garage. The mechanic says the piston rings must fit the cylinder walls within one-thousandth part of an inch. Even between friends there cannot be any variation if the motor is to run smoothly.

How then shall we expect that broad-mindedness shall rule in the realm of Christianity and morals? He that forsakes the truth of God, forsakes the God of truth.

The Bible is God's love letter. He gave it as an instruction book for life. If we follow the instructions and guidelines He lays down, we will be able to live life to the max and enjoy it rather than endure it. He is THE Owner and Manufacturer. He alone knows what makes us run at peak efficiency. Any deviation from the guidelines and principles outlined in the Owner's Manual, The Word of God, will severely hamper our physical, emotional and spiritual well-being. If all else fails, read and heed the Directions!

"Heavenly Father, Your Word is a lamp unto my feet and a light unto my path. Thank You for Your Owner's Manual. Show me where I have departed from Your guidelines. Give

me grace to follow Your instructions today to the letter so that I might do and be all You created me to do and be for Your glory and honor. Amen."

65

No, O people, the LORD has already told you what is good, and this is what He requires: to do what is right, to love mercy, and to walk humbly with your God.
—Micah 6:8 NLT

Most people are confused about what it takes to be a Christian. Some rock stars think that wearing a big old cross around your neck makes you a Christian. Others think Christianity is a long list of "do's & don'ts." Still others think that if they believe Jesus Christ is the Son of God, then they are Christians. Well, the devil believes that and trembles with fear (James 2:19). Is the devil a born-again Christian?

God is very clear about the essentials of Christianity. He gives three... only three... simple rules as to how His children should live if they claim to belong to Him.

1. **Do what is right.** That simply means following the commands and precepts outlined in God's Word. The Bible is pretty clear on how we should live and walk in faith. We just need to do it. The Holy Spirit living in us will let us know if we are doing what is right. When we are walking in truth, the peace of God will reign in our heart. When we step out of line, we lose our peace. The peace of God acts like an umpire

blowing the whistle on us by taking away our peace whenever we step out of bounds. **"And let the peace that comes from Christ rule in your hearts. For as members of one body you are all called to live in peace. And always be thankful"** (Colossians 3:15 NLT).

2. **Love mercy.** As Christians, we are called to glorify the Name of our Lord Jesus. To glorify means "to manifest the character and essence of." Since God is loving, kind, compassionate, just, truthful, longsuffering, merciful, etc., we should be as well. Since Jesus is our very life, we need to get out of His way and let Him live it through us. To love mercy simply means that we cut each other some slack just as Jesus does for us. **"Get rid of all bitterness, rage, anger, harsh words, and slander, as well as all types of malicious behavior. Instead, be kind to each other, tenderhearted, forgiving one another, just as God through Christ has forgiven you"** (Ephesians 4:31-32 NLT). We all fall down, but true Christians always get up. Sometimes we need a little help. The only time we should look down on someone is when we are reaching down to pick them up. Remember: The saints are just the sinners who fall down... AND get up.

3. **Walk humbly before the Lord.** When we do fall down, we confess to the Lord that we didn't follow His directions. Whenever the Lord comes and whispers in our ear, **"You have gotten off track. Let Me show you the way back,"** we humbly admit our sin and get back to following Him. Had we listened to the lord, we would not have fallen in the first place because He is able to keep us from falling. **"And now, all glory to God, Who is able to keep you from stumbling, and Who will bring you into His**

glorious presence innocent of sin and with great joy" (Jude 24 NLT)

"Father God, I want to glorify Your Name in all I do this day. Show me what's right and give me grace to do it. Help me to show mercy to others as You have been merciful to me. And when I mess up, humble Me with Your grace and goodness and get me back in line as quickly as possible. Amen."

66

The hopes of the godly result in happiness, but the expectations of the wicked are all in vain. —Proverbs 10:28 NLT

I like to go to the mall and sit on the benches and watch people. Have you ever noticed how sour and frustrated people look? You may see one happy person in a hundred, and it makes you wonder how deep that happiness really goes. I used to think everyone in the world was happy but me. Now I know better, and I guess misery loves company.

I used to be afraid of being happy. As a little boy, I used to get a whipping every time I had a good time. As most of you know, Superman... the real one... George Reeves... was my hero. I used to watch him on our old black and white TV. When commercials came on, I'd pin my cape on my T-shirt and fly around the yard. I loved Lois Lane, too. Every time she would get into trouble, I'd save her. One day I swooped down off the top of Mom's high poster bed to save Lois and knocked all the slats out onto the hardwood floor. Mama came in there and wore my tail out. I was having a ball and got a whipping for it.

One Friday when I was in the first grade, the teacher told us to pack up our books and wait for the bell to ring. She gave us a break by quitting a little early. Coupled with the fact that I was going to the football game that night made me very happy. I was sitting there humming the bridal song out of sheer joy... *"Here comes the bride... all dressed in white..."* when the teacher asked, *"Who's humming? I told you to be quiet."* I didn't even know I was humming. I was lost in my happiness. Then some little jerk beside me said, *"Kenny's humming."*

She said, *"Okay, Kenny, you stay after school until everyone else is gone."* See? I was happy again and got punished for it. My belief system... what I believed about God, myself, others and life in general was being formed. Part of my belief system came from what I observed and my life experiences. I began to observe that happiness was a signal to duck. Bad stuff came on the heels of joy. I learned that happiness was not okay. From the look on all those mall faces, a lot of people learned the same lesson.

So many people are frustrated today. Frustration and anger are synonymous. Frustration comes from unmet and unrealistic expectations. We expect life to be a certain way, and it's not. We expect people to treat us a certain way, and they don't. We become frustrated and angry because people and life are not meeting our needs. I'm going to frustrate you even more. They never will. They can't. They don't have the power to meet our needs. Only God has that power. Sure, He uses people to bless us and give us pleasure, but they are not the source. They are only the conduits of His blessings, and sometimes they get stopped up with sin and selfishness. We all do.

The Lord is the only One Who keeps all His promises. The only One Who never lets us down. The only One Who will never leave us nor forsake us. The only One Who can meet all of our needs. The only One Who loves us unconditionally all the time. How many of us can match that? Then why do we persist in expecting other people to do and be what only He can do and be?

It's time to give up hope, Beloved. No matter how good people are, they are just that... people. They don't have to power to love us unconditionally all the time. Only with the Lord, empowering them with His love, can they ever be used to meet our needs. We need to quit making idols out of people. Remember: an idol is anything we rely upon to meet our needs other than God.

Here's the pathway to happiness. The hopes of the godly lead to happiness. Put your hope in Him, not people. Love people, but don't expect them to be your all in all. Jesus is our all in all. May your soul wait only for Him. May all your expectations come from Him. If you do that, I expect joy will be spilling out all over you. Maybe some others might get doused in the meantime. Go for it! You've wasted enough time ducking. Don't worry. Be happy.

"Heavenly Father, help me stop expecting things from life and from people. Help me give all my expectations to You. Help my soul to wait only upon You. My hope and life is in You. Now that will make me happy. Amen."

67

And I want you to know, dear brothers and sisters, that everything that has happened to me here has helped to spread the Good News. For everyone here, including all the soldiers in the palace guard, knows that I am in chains because of Christ. And because of my imprisonment, many of the Christians here have gained confidence and become more bold in telling others about Christ.
—Philippians 1:12-14 NLT

On the way to the church this morning, I heard a radio broadcast of that old drama program, *Unshackled*. The program tells stories of people and their journeys to Christ. Most all of them relate how God turned apparent tragedy, rebellion and heartbreak into blessing. I was reminded of how God is always at work around us even though He works in ways we cannot see and understand at times.

During the war in Iraq, there was a terrible sandstorm. According to some locals, it was the worst in 100 years. A drenching rain followed the next day which bogged our troops down. The press was already wondering if the troops were in a "quagmire" and dire predictions of gloom and doom came from the left wing media. What they didn't report was that the next day, after the weather had cleared, the Marine group that was mired the worst looked out over the plain they were just about to cross. What did they see? Hundreds if not thousands of anti-tank and anti-personnel mines had been uncovered by the wind and then washed off by the rain. If they had proceeded as planned, many lives would have undoubtedly been lost. As it was, they simply drove around them and let the demolition teams destroy them.

For those who love God and are called to His purposes, all things work together for our good and His glory (Romans 8:28). That's why we should be thankful for all the things that God allows to touch our lives... good, bad or ugly. He has a plan. He loves us. He knows what's best for us although what's best sometimes comes dressed in the most repulsive clothes... like cancer, lost jobs and opportunities, and the storms of life. God is able to make something beautiful out of the ugliest of circumstances. How we view those storms is our choice. We can choose to embrace the silver lining behind the cloud, or we can choose to curse the wind, rain and sand.

Winds of adversity make eagles soar higher and higher. Those same winds can also expose the land mines in our lives that seek to blow us apart. Be thankful that God not only calms storms but stirs them up as well.

"Heavenly Father, forgive me for always asking You to make my life more comfortable when what You really desire is to make me more like You in every way. Thank You for the storms in my life today. Use them to blow away everything in my life that's not like You. Thanks. Amen."

68

Trust in the LORD with all your heart; do not depend on your own understanding. —Proverbs 3:5 NLT

Would you indulge me today and let me simply share some thoughts about my relationship with the Lord. This thought is for me more than you. I just need to verbalize some things I've been mulling over for a while. Thanks in advance for listening.

I'm a thinker-feeler. I know people are generally one or the other, but God has blessed me (or cursed me, only He knows) with both. I think about things that probably no one else ever thinks about. I feel things very, very deeply. I take things very, very personally. I think about the truth, the Word of God, and know in my mind without a shadow of doubt that what God says is absolutely pure and without error. But I don't always feel, or experience, that truth in my emotions. I want to. I've always wanted to. It's one thing to know in your mind that you are unconditionally loved and forgiven. It's quite another to *feel* loved and forgiven. You know what I mean?

Wanda and I went to experience the Toronto Blessing at the Toronto Airport Christian Fellowship about three years ago. I wanted to go experience the titillation of a spiritual blessing. I really wanted God to knock me on the floor, heal all my hurts and wounds, meet all my needs, and give me a warm fuzzy feeling that would last a lifetime. It didn't work.

I've come to believe that emotions make wonderful servants, but terrible masters. The Word of God tells me to walk by faith and in the Spirit, not by my feelings. Feelings lie. They are not reliable indicators of the truth. Let me illustrate. One night I went frog hunting in a creek. I waded in the water looking for frogs on sand bars. Then I spied a big old water moccasin lying on the bank. Fear gripped my emotions as I stood motionless in the water. As I was pondering my next move, a stick came floating down the creek and hit me in the back of the leg. I didn't catch the branch of that tree on the way up, but I caught it on the way down. I just knew that his brother had ambushed me from the rear and bit me on the back of the leg. I just knew I had only minutes to live. I ran away from that creek as fast as I could with my emotions running at a 12 on a scale of 10. When I finally thought I was safe, I pulled up my britches' leg and looked for the fang marks. There were two little black specks. My emotions jumped to 15. Then my frog hunting partner reached over and brushed the specks away. It was dirt. I hadn't been bitten at all, but my emotions weren't buying it.

My mind, which believed at level 10 that I had been bitten, immediately dropped back down to one. I knew in my mind that I had not been bitten. My emotions, in spite of the truth, still hovered around 9. See what I mean? Because my emotions have a hard time believing, does that make the truth any less valid? No. So what do we need to listen to... fact or feeling?

Do you think Jesus really felt like going to the cross? Do you think it felt good to be betrayed, rejected and slandered? What if Jesus had based His actions upon His feelings? What would have become of you and me?

When I coached football, we would look for kids to cover kickoffs who would seek out and destroy the ball carrier.

Kids who would have total disregard for their own safety. Kids who cared about one thing and one thing alone... tackle the ball carrier as quickly as possible. We looked for kids with "reckless abandon." Nothing else mattered but their mission. That was the secret to Jesus' successful mission of redeeming us by His atonement. Nothing else mattered to Him but the Father's will and purpose. No pain. No discomfort. No feeling. Nothing could distract Him from what Father had sent Him to do.

I'm ashamed to say that my life is filled with distractions. I let hurt feelings paralyze me from accomplishing my mission. I too often care more for my comfort than I do about the eternal needs of others and His will for my life. I'm more prone to seek an experience than obedience to His call upon my life. I am not recklessly abandoned to His will. In light of His sacrifice for me, nothing I do can be considered a sacrifice. I hope and pray to come to the place where I can pray as Paul did... *"I eagerly expect and hope that I will in no way be ashamed, but will have sufficient courage so that now as always Christ will be exalted in my body, whether by life or by death"* (Philippians 1:20 NIV).

Therefore, I beseech you, Beloved, in light of His love, grace and mercy that we become "recklessly abandoned" to Him. He is truly worthy!

"Lord, give me grace this day to be recklessly abandoned to You. May I tackle the enemy and stop him dead in his tracks. May I be light and salt in the world today. I will trust You today... feelings or not! It feels good to walk in faith. Thanks. Amen."

69

I strain to reach the end of the race and receive the prize for which God, through Christ Jesus, is calling us up to heaven. —Philippians 3:14 NLT

Ever heard of "heartbreak hill"? I've seen long-distance foot races where the last few hundred yards are all uphill. When a runner reaches the homestretch and sees that hill in front of him, his heart breaks, his spirit is crushed and his body cries, "NO!" It takes every ounce of determination he can muster to finish the race. Every thing inside of him is screaming for him to quit, but he finds the energy for one more step... then another... and another until at last he crosses the finish-line. Hallelujah! A desire fulfilled is sweet to the soul (Proverbs 13:19).

In my race to win the prize for which Christ Jesus has called me heavenward, I have finally come to heartbreak hill. During this fifty plus year marathon, I've run through some cool shady spots as well as some deserts, mountains and valleys. God has run with me all the way, although at times, I was unaware of His presence. Sweat, pain, toil and tears have a way of blinding us to the reality of His nearness. But looking back on my race, I see now how loving and faithful He's been. There have been times when I've been unfaithful, but He remained faithful. There have been times when I believed men rather than God because I craved their acceptance over His grace and truth. I've taken many a wrong road because I neglected to seek His wisdom and guidance. Nevertheless, He was always there to gently guide me back on the right path whenever I cried out, *"Lord, I'm lost again. Please help me!"* He is so good. There are not enough books, paper and ink in the world to express how great, loving, kind, faithful, generous, merciful... I could go on and fill the rest of this book with nothing more than His attributes. He is everything I need. I guess that's why He calls Himself, "I AM."

As I near the end of my race, my greatest challenge lies before me. I've lived long enough to have heard most of the philosophies about the proper way to run this race called life. Many of those I've believed and trusted have put me in great bondage. The heartbreak in my hill is intensified by the fact that God is asking me to give up most everything I've ever believed about how He relates to me, not how I relate to Him. I know that God wants me to tell everyone the Good News that He loves them... period. They don't have to do anything to earn it. Jesus paid the bill. When we trust Him as Lord and Savior, we don't have to keep paying our sin debt anymore. We are free to be who He created us to be. But as in days of old, religion still fights that message tooth and nail. Religion wants to keep us in bondage so it can control us and get us to do what will benefit its own selfish agenda. Religion glorifies man. True Christianity glorifies God. And the battle rages on.

Allow me to elaborate. I was told at a young age that accepting what Jesus did for me on the Cross was the only way I could be saved. I couldn't save myself. I had to let Jesus save me. But once I trusted in Christ for my salvation, I was told by the institution of the church that I had better work my rear end off if wanted to keep it. In other words, the message I perceived was that God's love was conditional.

If I didn't make Him mad, make Him look bad, or ever sin, then He would love me and keep His end of the bargain. But woe be unto me if I ever slipped up and failed.

Religion will deny that it preaches this doctrine, but it does. For instance, a person is saved, and the first verse we give him to memorize is I John 1:9... *"If we confess our sins, He is faithful and just to forgive us our sins and cleanse us from all unrighteousness."* We tell him, *"Now listen. You are not perfect like Jesus. You are going to sin. When you do, here's the bar of soap to get you clean so He will forgive you. You must stay clean if you want to be a child of God."*

Beloved, Jesus made me clean by His blood. His blood cleansed me the day I surrendered to Him as Lord and Savior. He gave me life... His Life. I was dead before that. *"You were dead because of your sins and because your sinful nature was not yet cut away. Then God made you alive with Christ. He forgave ALL our sins. He canceled the record that contained the charges against us. He took it and destroyed it by nailing it to Christ's cross"* (Colossians 2:13-15 NLT). Then look what happened... *"What this means is that those who become Christians become new persons. They are not the same anymore, for the old life is gone. A new life has begun!"* (2 Corinthians 5:16-17 NLT).

God loves sinners. He hates sin. He has no problem separating the two. He can still love us even when we sin. What religion has told us, and I have been a participant much to my chagrin, is this... *"Come out from among them and be separate. A little leaven leavens the whole lump. Be holy for I am holy. Only the pure in heart will see God. Be perfect even as your Father in heaven is perfect."* What religion doesn't tell you is that Jesus is your righteousness, your holiness, your perfection, your purity, your life, your all in all. By His sacrifice, He has made perfect forever those of us who are in the process of being made holy (Hebrews 10:14). God has forgiven us of ALL our sins... past, present and future. If I am a new creation and old things have passed away, nothing can ever change that. Nothing can ever separate me from His love. I am His child forever. *"For I am persuaded that neither death nor life, nor angels nor principalities nor powers, nor things present nor things to come, nor height nor depth, nor any other created thing, shall be able to separate us from the love of God which is in Christ Jesus our Lord"* (Rom 8:38-39 NKJV).

In the past, I have bought into religion's philosophy that says that God needs me to protect His reputation. Religion says that I must not tell people that God loves them unconditionally and that nothing can thwart His love for them. If you don't keep telling people how sinful they are, then they will take advantage of God's grace and go wild with sin giving God a bad reputation. Beloved, God's reputation doesn't need defending anymore than a lion needs protection from a mouse.

Religion has portrayed a God that is only concerned about Himself and cares more for His reputation than the welfare of His children. That is the lie that came out of the Garden of Eden and is still propagated today. The serpent told Eve that God was keeping the good stuff for Himself. He told her that God didn't want her to eat the forbidden fruit because He was jealous of her knowing as much as He did. Religion is a major tool of the devil.

Beloved, God is not concerned with His reputation. Philippians 2:7 tells us that Jesus made Himself of no reputation. He gave up heaven's glory to come to earth to be despised and rejected, humiliated and crucified for you and me. How self-less is that? When Jesus died on the Cross, He asked His Father to forgive those who crucified Him because they didn't know what they were doing. Does that sound like a God on an ego trip?

If you have trusted Christ as your Lord and Savior, God is for you. He is on your side. He believes in you. He pulls for you. Your picture is on His refrigerator. He jumps up and down and hollers when you hit a homerun, and He has a pocketful of life-savers when you strike out. He thinks you're the best thing since sliced bread. You are the apple of His eye. He is crazy about You. What's not to love about a God like that? And that is what He is really like.

Beloved, God is asking me to shed all my old false philosophies about Who He really is. By doing so, the religious community will rise up and call me names... bad names like heretic, yellow-bellied liberal... you get the picture. Some of those are the best friends I have. That is the heartbreak in my hill. I like being accepted by people just like we all do, but I'm so close to the finish line now, I can almost see His face. What I see gives me the strength and courage to take one more step, and with every step, the prize gets a little closer. If the religion race has taken its toll on you, too, then why don't you step out and join me. I'd enjoy the company.

"Heavenly Father, thanks for the strength to run the race and finish the course. Thanks for the faith You've given me that keeps me going when I want to quit. I know that You ran the race before me and are running the race with me. I also know that You will be at the finish line to greet me when I break the tape. I think I'm going to sprint the rest of the way. May this leg of the race bring glory and honor to You, Lord. Amen."

70

My cup runneth over. —Psalm 23:5 KJV

Did you know that the Truth, in and of itself, will not set you free? The Bible does not claim that the Truth will set you free. Jesus said, **"And you shall *know* the truth, and the truth shall make you free."** (John 8:32 NKJV). The Greek word for "know" is *ginosko* which basically means *"to understand; to have experiential knowledge of."*

Allow me to illustrate. I make the best instant mashed potatoes. They are simple and easy to make and taste just as good as the real thing to me. You know how to make them, don't you? You boil water and add a little salt. When the water begins to boil, you take it off the heat and add some milk and the instant potato flakes. Then you whip'em up until they are creamy and fluffy. Yum-yum. But you don't make instant cream potatoes without a shirt on. One day as I was whipping them up, a glob of potatoes splattered on my chest. Wow! I brushed it off as quickly as I could but in so doing my spoon hand jerked and splattered hot potatoes all over my chest. Double WOW! I had water blisters on my chest for days.

Now I can tell you the truth about making instant mashed potatoes without a shirt, but you won't really *know* the truth like I do until you've done the same thing. I *know* what hot mashed potatoes will do to a shirtless chest. Until you have experienced it, you don't know. Do you think I'll ever make instant mashed potatoes again without a shirt? I don't think so.

The Truth of God's Word is like that. It has to be experienced before it will set you free. Until the Truth is clung to, relied upon and totally trusted in, it will never become effectual in your life. But once you've been burned by your slackness, no one will ever have to tell you again to keep your shirt on. Know what I mean?

God made people like cups to be filled with His Truth to overflowing so that His Truth will not only benefit us but those upon whom we overflow. But here's the problem. There are not many *ginosko* cups out there.

Some are like cups turned upside down... kinda like the way you turn your coffee cup at a restaurant when you don't want any coffee. God's Truth is like crystal clear water. He wants His crystal clear Truth to fill us all to overflowing. However, some cups are turned upside down and no matter how much Truth is poured on them, none ever gets inside. They are not having any.

Others are like cups with a hole in the bottom. They take in the Truth and may even delight in it, but they don't retain very much at all. They don't apply it. They just listen to it. Therefore, they never grow very much in the grace and knowledge of our Lord Jesus and end up empty.

Still others are like cups with mud on the bottom. The mud represents their own opinions about what the Truth is. If the clear Truth of God's Word contradicts what they have made up their minds to believe, they reject it. The water becomes muddy, and they become confused. They even contradict themselves when they try to explain what they believe to be the Truth.

The kind of cup that God uses is the one that is turned right side up with no holes... empty of any pre-conceived notions and squeaky clean. These cups receive the Truth joyfully and keep themselves under the spout where the glory comes out. They fill up quickly and pour themselves out on those around them so that they can be filled with more Truth.

What about your cup? Could it be time for you to turn over and ask the Lord to mend and clean you so that you can be a vessel unto honor and set apart for His glory?

"Heavenly Father, mend and clean my cup today. Pour Yourself into me until I can't hold all of You. Then spill out onto those You bring across my path today. Amen."

71

Give thanks to the LORD, for He is good! His faithful love endures forever. —Psalm 136:1 NLT

We often learn the most from our children. Some time ago, I heard about a dad that punished his three year old daughter for wasting a roll of gold wrapping paper. Money was tight, and he became infuriated when the child tried to decorate a box to put under the tree. Nevertheless, the little girl brought the gift to her father on Christmas morning and said, *"This is for you Daddy!"*

He was embarrassed by his earlier overreaction, but his anger flared again when he found that the box was empty. He yelled at her, *"Don't you know that when you give someone a present there is supposed to be something inside of it?"*

The little girl looked up at him with tears in her eyes and said, *"Oh Daddy, it's not empty. I blew kisses into the box, all for you Daddy."* The father was crushed. He put his arms around his little girl and begged for her forgiveness. I was told that he kept that gold box by his bed for years. Whenever he felt discouraged, he would take out an imaginary kiss and remember the love of the child who had put it there. In a real sense, each of us as a parent has been given a gold container filled with unconditional love and kisses from our children. There is no more precious possession anyone could hold.

Our Father gave us the greatest gift of all... love, forgiveness and salvation... wrapped up in the most expensive wrapping paper... His only begotten Son. If He gave us the best, do you think He will not give us the rest. Father God's love endures forever. It is an everlasting love that does not fluctuate with our moods. Like Jesus, Himself, it is the same yesterday, today and forever.

God has blessed us beyond our comprehension. As a Dad, I know of nothing that blesses my heart more than when my children tell me, *"Dad, I love you."* Why don't we bless Him today.

"Father, words can't begin to express how much I love You today. Thank You for my Lord Jesus Who loved me so much that He took my place on the Cross. I should have been nailed there, not Him. Keep me ever mindful that I am crucified with You, Lord Jesus, and I no longer live, but You live in Me. Lord, live full and free in me this day. Thanks for the gift of Your love which endures forever. Nobody ever loved me like You do. May I be a blessing to You all day long. I love You, too. Amen."

72

Wait for the Lord; be strong and take heart and wait for the LORD. —Psalm 27:14

Have you ever poured your heart out to God in desperation and all you heard was the deafening roar of silence? When Lazarus got sick, Mary and Martha sent word by messenger for Jesus to come and heal their brother. Upon receiving the message, Jesus stayed where He was for two more days. Why did Jesus do that? Because His father told Him to do that. He always waited for His Father's instructions. Jesus never made a move or said a word without first hearing from His Father. **"But I do nothing without consulting the Father. I judge as I am told. And My judgment is absolutely just, because it is according to the will of God Who sent Me; it is not merely My own"** (John 5:30 NLT).

Do we follow Christ's example? Do we wait on Him to instruct us as to when, where and how to do or say what He desires? Or do we become frustrated because of His silence and take matters into our own hands? I have learned one thing from experience. If you lag behind in obeying the Lord, you may miss out on a few blessings. But if you run ahead of Him before He gives you His orders, you will run smack dab into trouble. After years of running into brick walls and scores of bloody noses, I have learned to wait on Him even when everyone around me is clamoring for me to DO SOMETHING!

We tend to think that God's silence shows that our request is wrong or sinful, and sometimes they are. However, there are times when God's silence is His answer. Think about it. Has there ever been a time in the past when you prayed for something and God answered with silence? Then years later you saw your prayer answered in a much bigger way than you ever dreamed? That's what happened with Mary and Martha. They asked Jesus to come and heal their brother. Their request was met with silence. Four days later, a loud, thunderous answer they never even dreamed of came walking out of a tomb.

If sin or wrong motives are not our problem, then God's silence is a badge of honor. He believes in us. He can trust us with a bigger revelation of Himself and His purposes than we ever imagined. If He only gives us a visible answer to prayer that means He cannot trust us yet.

I had a dream one time about a party in a big ballroom. I saw Jesus come through the door. He came up to this man and put His arm around His shoulder and began talking to him as they walked around the room. I so wanted Jesus to put His arm around me and talk to me. As Jesus walked by, our eyes met. He winked at me and kept walking. That wink spoke to my spirit. I didn't understand it then, but I think I do now. I believe Jesus was saying, "**I love this young man, but I cannot trust him with Kingdom matters yet. He has not grown to the place where His faith will survive without visible evidence. I'm looking for people whose faith will flourish even in the absence of any visible manifestation, or in the void of silence, because they simply trust Me and My character. My pleasure and My purposes are all that matter to them. My wink was affirmation that I think you are able to handle a bigger revelation.**"

Jesus told Thomas, **"Thomas you have put your hand in My side and felt the nail prints in My hands. Now you believe. But blessed are those who have not seen and still believe"** (John 20:29). As long as we think that God only blesses us through tangible answered prayer, then He will never give us the greater blessing of silence. God will answer our prayers and give us the blessings we want if we won't go any farther, but His silence is His invitation to bring us into a vastly deeper understanding of Himself.

Wait on the Lord, Beloved. When things appear dark and hopeless, sit silently and wait. Listen intently. Keep quiet in the dark. Darkness is not a time for talking. It is a time for waiting... watching... listening. When the Lord breaks the silence, it will be worth the wait!

"Father God, I'm afraid of the dark. I don't like it when you stop talking. But I know in my heart that You are still here with me even in the silent darkness. You are faithful. You use the dark silence to teach me to be faithful like You. Don't turn on the light until I'm ready to shine even if I cry and beg you to do so. I'm waiting while You are strengthening me. Thanks for not giving up on me. Amen."

73

The steps of the godly are directed by the LORD. He delights in every detail of their lives. —Psalm 37:23 NLT

Major Ian Thomas once said that the way God leads His children is something like this: *"He starts them out at point A, but before they go very far, they are diverted to point B. Just before they reach point B, the Lord diverts them again, and they wind up at point C. God wanted them at point C all along, but He had to take them through the experiences of points A and B in order to get them where He wanted them."* The Major is right on. I can see that pattern throughout my entire life. What about you?

A long time ago, I told the Lord that I did not ever want to preach/teach anything that I had not experienced personally. Boy, has there ever been times I wished I had never told Him that. God takes us seriously. He takes our word a lot more seriously than we take His. And how faithful He has been to do what I have asked Him to do.

When I made that request, I had visions of being just like Jesus... loving, kind, patient, joyful, authoritative, just, righteous, etc. I think Paul made the same request I made, but he understood better than I did what it takes to get the "good stuff." ***"I want to know Christ and the power of His resurrection and the fellowship of sharing in His suffer-***

ings, becoming like Him in His death, and so, somehow, to attain to the resurrection from the dead" (Philippians 3:10-11 NIV). Resurrection comes after death... not before. What is blocking the "good stuff" is our old unsurrendered soul with its self-centered agenda. The main lie of the devil is that we can attain to the resurrection and by-pass the cross. That's an impossibility. Remember when the devil told Jesus in Matthew chapter 4 that he would give Him all the kingdoms of the world if He would bow down and worship him? What the devil was saying is this: *"Jesus, You don't have to go to the cross to get all the 'good stuff'."* That's the same lie he is perpetrating today.

The fellowship of His sufferings is absolutely essential to burn out the dross in our souls so that the Lord, Who is our Life, can come shining through. There is no crown without the Cross. No glory without the gore. No resurrection without a death. No power without suffering.

That is why God has to take us through points A, B, and sometimes all the way through Z to get us to the place where He is our all in all. If we truly want to be like Jesus Who gave His life that we might live, then we must concur with Paul when he says... *"For we who are alive are always being given over to death for Jesus' sake, so that His life may be revealed in our mortal body. So then, death is at work in us, but life is at work in you"* (2 Corinthians 4:11-12 NIV).

Jesus wants to live and love through us to save a lost and dying world. Get the point?

"Father, keep me pointed in the right direction. I have a tendency to jump from A to Z without learning the lessons from B to Y. I give my life to You anew today. Keep my life in alphabetical order for Your glory. I love You. Amen."

74

*Forgetting the past and looking forward to
what lies ahead...* —Philippians 3:13 NLT

I constantly hear people say, *"Suppose I had better parents... What if I had been given a chance... If only this terrible tragedy had not happened to me..."* Then they turn right around and tell me that all that stuff doesn't matter. It's in the past. My next question is this: *If it's in the past and you've dealt with it, then why are you still talking about it?*

We all have stuff in our past. We live in a fallen, imperfect world. God created us to live in a perfect world. We are not suited to the world in which we live. All creation groans along with us as we wait in anticipation of the day when the Lord Jesus will restore what man's disobedience and satan's rebellion have done to God's original perfect order. In the meantime, **"God has rescued us from the one who rules in the kingdom of darkness, and He has brought us into the Kingdom of His dear Son"** (Colossians 1:13 NLT). By His blood, He has saved us out of the condemnation of the world. By His grace, He gives us the desire and power to do His will and fulfill our destiny regardless of our past.

God's Word tells us that He has sovereignly orchestrated all the events of our lives. All things work together for our good and His glory if we love Him and are called according to

His purpose, not ours (Romans 8:28). I've known people who had terrible home situations... addictions, abuse, neglect... who were overcomers and lived dynamic Christian lives. I'm also familiar with people who had wonderful Christian homes who turned out to be rebels. Our attitude determines our altitude. Philippians 2:5 tells us that we should have the attitude of Christ. He had a lot going against Him, but He didn't become bitter. His life and attitude of joyful submission to His Father made us better. He chose to endure this imperfect world and die in our place. Bless His holy name that He did.

All our pain, sorrow, hurt, wounds and scars are part of the lyrics of the song God has given us to sing. But we get to write the melody. We can write a funeral dirge and trudge into the pit of despair and hopelessness, or we can write a joyful tune and dance gleefully in the presence of the King. The choice is ours.

"He has given me a new song to sing, a hymn of praise to our God. Many will see what He has done and be astounded. They will put their trust in the LORD" (Psalm 40:3 NLT). Okay, Beloved, name that tune!

"Heavenly Father, I realize now that I am who I am because of what has happened to me. When I reflect upon my past, I sometimes become bitter, and sometimes I become better. A lot of the good things in me... patience, honesty, integrity, love and mercy... came as a result of some of the really bad things I had to endure. Help me to see that grinding stones either grind me down or polish me. My attitude and the choices I make determine whether I shine or scuff. Polish me today as I dance my way home to You. Amen."

75

But even the best of these years are filled with pain and trouble; soon they disappear, and we are gone. Teach us to make the most of our time, so that we may grow in wisdom.
—Psalm 90:10 & 12 NLT

Priorities. How quickly we allow our priorities to get messed up. We worry about what people think about us when, in actuality, we flatter ourselves with the idea that people care enough to even think about us at all. We think that if we don't find a cure for our slice, make it to the top of corporate ladder, make more money than Bill Gates, get everyone in the world to agree with us, and be in control of every person and circumstance in our lives then we are worthless.

God has ways of prioritizing our priorities. In March of 1989, we moved to Shelby to win the world to Jesus. I knew God needed me to convert everyone in Cleveland County, North Carolina, America and the uttermost parts of the earth. I was unable to see how the Lord had made it as long as He had without me. Since I had finished seminary and was fully equipped, I was ready to give the final impetus for moving His Kingdom to earth just as it was in heaven. I was focused, which is another word for "tunnel-vision." That's when you lose sight of His priorities because yours keep getting in the way.

Jesus... My Final Answer

For the first few months, my agenda was going quite well. The church was growing. The budget was up. People were pleased with me. I could see the Kingdom coming. Then Wanda went for her first routine mammogram. She was diagnosed with *intraductile carcinoma insitu*... a fancy term for breast cancer. In a moment... one silly little old moment... my priorities took a 180 degree turn. All of a sudden, I didn't care if the Kingdom ever came. My kingdom was crumbling, and I couldn't do a thing about it. I couldn't care less what people thought about me, or how well the church was going, or that I was God's most valuable player. I came to the stark realization that I might lose the love of my life... a love that had fallen far down my list of priorities in my quest to win the world for Jesus.

That event was a wake-up call for me. Nothing in the whole world mattered to me but keeping my wife, my friend, my lover with me. I couldn't imagine my life without her. I didn't even know if I had a life apart from her. But God was merciful and gracious. He brought us both through that ordeal and put things in proper perspective for me... for a while. It wasn't long until I was right back at it... building *my* kingdom in His Name.

I can't tell you how many times I've read Ecclesiastes. It speaks volumes to me. Solomon knew all about priorities. He had experienced it all... fame, power, position, wealth. At the end of his life, he came to one conclusion. All was vanity... a chasing after the wind. We never catch the wind, or control it, and yet we spend our lives chasing it.

As I write this chapter, my mom is in the hospital. Her health has been deteriorating for the last few months. I don't know what the future holds for her, but the prognosis is not promising. I've never lost a parent, a sibling, a wife, or a child. Losing people who are close to you happens to other people, not me. God is prioritizing my priorities once again.

Jesus... My Final Answer

When all is said and done, and you come to the end of life, there are only three things that are going to matter to you: your faith, your family, and your friends. I've said that at most every funeral I've ever preached, but it's hitting home now. Why do we memorize Scripture? Why do we go to seminars? Why do we constantly try to learn more and more about God and never come to know Him intimately? We become so enamored with the means that we lose sight of the end. I don't believe that God put us here to learn a bunch of facts about Him. I think God put us here to love Him and one another so much that those who don't know Him would be attracted to Him because of our love. God put us here to enjoy Him and His blessings, not just to endure Him.

When you get ready to go meet Him face to face, and all of us will, your faith is all you will have to hold on to. It won't matter how much Scripture you've memorized, or how many times you attended church, or how many degrees you have on your wall. All that will matter is this: Did you keep the faith? Did you finish the course? Did you trust Jesus for your salvation and eternal destiny rather than your own self-righteous works? Did you enjoy the family God gave you to love, both biological and spiritual? Did you treasure the friends He provided for you to make your journey a little easier? Did you revel in the fullness of the life He gave you?

I don't know about you, but I'm tired of the performance treadmill. I'm tired of trying to be God's MVP. That's a joke. God needs me about as much as a submarine needs a screen door. But He sure does love me. All He wants is for me to trust Him and love Him back. He even gives me friends like you to love me, too. He's got my attention again. This time, I don't plan for Him to lose it.

"Heavenly Father, our days fly by like a weaver's shuttle. If we live a hundred years on this earth, it will be a mere

drop in the sea of eternity. Lord, please don't let me waste my life on things that don't really matter. Don't let me lose sight of Your priorities for my life... faith, family and friends. You have given me all things to enjoy. I've wasted too much time already. Today I choose to enjoy You, my family and my friends. Nothing else really matters, does it? Amen."

76

Always learning but never able to acknowledge the truth.
—2 Timothy 3:7 NIV

I've spent my entire life learning. I have a bachelor's degree and two master's degrees and have been to more seminars and read more books than I can count. As I become more and more chronologically gifted, I'm still learning. I'm learning that the most important lessons do not come from textbooks and classrooms. They come from life. I'm sorry to say that I've run right by some of life's greatest lessons in pursuit of knowledge. I've come to the place where knowing what to do must be translated into doing what I know. A fellow once told me that it's what you learn after you know it all that really counts. I never understood until now how right he was. Today, I want to share with you some things I've learned after I learned it all.

   I've learned... that the best classroom in the world is at the feet of an elderly person.
   I've learned... that when you're in love, it shows.
   I've learned... that just one person saying to me, *"You've made my day!"* makes my day.
   I've learned... that having a child fall asleep in your arms is one of the most peaceful feelings in the world.

Jesus... My Final Answer

I've learned... that being kind is more important that being right.

I've learned... that you should never say "no" to a gift from a child.

I've learned... that I can always pray for someone when I don't have the strength to help him in some other way.

I've learned... that no matter how serious your life requires you to be, everyone needs a friend to act goofy with.

I've learned... that sometimes all a person needs is a hand to hold and a heart to understand.

I've learned... that watching my Dad love my Mom when I was small did wonders for me now that I'm big and a husband and father myself.

I've learned... that life is like a roll of toilet paper. The closer it gets to the end, the faster it goes.

I've learned... that we should be glad God doesn't give us everything we ask for.

I've learned... that money doesn't buy class.

I've learned... that it's those small daily happenings that make life so spectacular.

I've learned... that under everyone's hard shell is someone who wants to be appreciated and loved.

I've learned... that the Lord didn't do it all in one day. What makes me think I can?

I've learned... that to ignore the facts does not change the facts.

I've learned... that when you plan to get even with someone, you are only letting that person continue to hurt you.

I've learned... that love, not time, heals all wounds.

I've learned... that the easiest way for me to grow as a person is to surround myself with people smarter than I am.

I've learned... that everyone you meet deserves to be greeted with a smile.

I've learned... that there's nothing sweeter than sleeping with your babies and feeling their breath on your cheeks.

I've learned... that no one is perfect until you fall in love with them.

I've learned... that life is tough, but I'm tougher.

I've learned... that opportunities are never lost; someone will take the ones you miss.

I've learned... that when you harbor bitterness, happiness will dock elsewhere.

I've learned... that I wish I could have told that very special person that I love them one more time before they passed away.

I've learned... that one should keep his words both soft and tender, because tomorrow he may have to eat them.

I've learned... that a smile is an inexpensive way to improve your looks.

I've learned... that I can't choose how I feel, but I can choose what to do about it.

I've learned... that when your newly born child holds your little finger in his fist, you're hooked for life.

I've learned... that everyone wants to live on top of the mountain, but all the happiness and growth occurs while you're climbing it.

I've learned... that it is best to give advice in only two circumstances; when it is requested and when it is a life threatening situation.

I've learned... that the less time I have to work with, the more things I get done.

And I'm still learning day by day by the grace and mercy of God. I've learned that youth is wasted on the young and that experience is like a comb you get after you are bald. I would like to have learned all these precious truths when I was young and energetic enough to implement and enjoy them. But hey, it's never to late. I've learned that it's never too late to start living. I've learned that it's a waste of time to learn if you never get around to applying it. Now, let that be a lesson to you!

"Heavenly Father, You have taught me so much. A lot of the best things I've learned came from the School of Hard Knocks. I know I griped about the assignments You made to me during those classes, but I am better and stronger for it. One thing I've especially learned... You are the best, most patient, most gracious, most loving, most wise Teacher ever. And I love You. Amen."

Printed in the United States
200094BV00002B/637-660/A